A WALK ON THE SOUTH SIDE

First published in 2010 by
Morrigan New Century
Killala, Co. Mayo, Ireland
morriganbooks@gmail.com

The illustration on page 12 is from a painting by Ann Kennedy.

A CIP catalogue record for this work is available
from The British Library.

ISBN 978 0 907677 39 0

Origination and Design by
Hayes Design, St Leonards on Sea, Sussex, England.

Printed in the UK by Ashford Colour Press.

A Walk On
THE SOUTH SIDE

CONAN KENNEDY

MORRIGAN

Google says...

Dún Laoghaire or **Dún Laoire** (Irish pronunciation: [d̪ˠuːn̪ˠ ˈt̪ʲeːɾʲə]), Anglicised as **Dunleary** (English pronunciation: /dʌn ˈlɪəri/), is a suburban seaside town and county seat of Dun Laoghaire-Rathdown County, Ireland.

The town is situated some 12 kilometres south of Dublin city centre, and is a major port of entry from Great Britain.

This article **may require cleanup to meet Wikipedia's quality standards**. Please improve this article if you can.

Ok, I'll try.

LANSDOWNE, KILLINEY ROAD

"**J**UST AS WELL they didn't meet in *The Bleeding Horse*". Such was the son Hugo's comment when I told him my own parents had met in Lansdowne Tennis Club. Hence the reason they called their house *Lansdowne*. That house was their life. Married in 1941, they never lived anywhere else as a married couple. And rarely went on holidays. Though I do remember them once taking my older sister and myself to a rented holiday cottage in Brittas Bay. That was about it, holiday wise. They were a quiet and secretive couple, very hard to know.

I am a novelist, and on top of that I am their son...but I never understood them. And still don't. They didn't seem to have any friends. I rarely remember people calling. Which was a pity. My mother had good china and silver teapots and the like, and she kept the house very well, quite prepared for visitors. And we had a maid.

Lansdowne is on Killiney Road, more or less opposite the cul de sac known as Killiney Grove. Pushing the word *grove* a bit, those one and a half miserable trees poking out of tarmac. But a gesture I suppose.

The parents' house was new when they moved in, a Mr Conway had built it and the two others alongside. The site was really just the edge of a field by the road. There were no houses opposite on the left hand side of Killiney Road in those days. I was born in this house. A home birth. But not for trendy reasons. In those days it was the normal thing. In fact the trendy thing for the middleclasses then was to be born in a nursing home. Trendiness tends to be based on having money, being different to the norm. For no particular practical reason.

Dr Wright came over from Dalkey to deliver me. Dr Wright was son of an earlier Dr Wright, one of those old doctoring families that don't seem to have continued to our times. The earlier edition had been my mother's doctor as a child. They lived in Ulverton Road, but had lands behind. 'Dr Wright's Field'. This is now the site of Ormeau Park. Which… and here comes the really uninteresting bit, was built by a Mr Martin from Belfast who's grandson's name is mentioned most mornings on RTÉ's *Morning Ireland*. 'And the editor was Niall Martin'.

God my mind is cluttered

Anyway, Dr Wright bicycled over 'with a bag of rusty tools", or so my father said. But my father said things like that. When he spoke at all. A humourous person, he lived in the silent audience of life, as someone watching bad comedians. But sometimes he found it funny, and laughed. Generally though it was a quiet house. Very quiet. There was a rhythm. Dargle Laundry in Bray collected sheets, for laundering. Grimes in Dalkey delivered meat, by bicycle. And milk was delivered on a cart from Wilkie's Farm in Saval Park Road. And no, I am not one hundred and eight. It was all just very different then. The times and the house itself. The picture opposite shows it as it was for the sixty years of my parents' ownership, an auctioneer's shot of the place just before it was sold. But later it was changed. Extended and modernised. Electric gates. And all. Amazing how for only a hundred thousand euro or so it's possible to remove every last vestige of character from a house.

As a child I looked out those windows across fields full of haystacks, back and front. And the grazing of cows, the seasons changing, all that. To the back was Wilkie's Field, now the site of Ballinclea Heights. And beyond that the hill known locally then as 'the rocks'. Officially it's Roches Hill. The same Roches as in Rochestown Avenue. I don't think there was any bloke called *Roche* involved in this at all. And believe the name derives from an old French word for *rocks*. Sensible enough. This was all rocky countryside. With a plethora of Carraig roads and Corrig roads and…Rock roads.

That small window in the centre of the front of the house was my bedroom. I could see to Dublin Bay from there. Foghorns blared, and east winds blew in the smell of the sea. That bay seemed to be nearer then. All changed now. The window immediately to the left of mine was the bedroom of my sister Louise Kennedy. An international swimmer, she was later to be a well known swimming teacher around Dún Laoghaire. She died suddenly and young. I record her here. Unmarried, with no children, she is forgotten otherwise. My parents too are both gone to their reward now. My mother to Glasnevin to the Roman Catholic grave of her own people. And my father to 'the Protestant side' of Deans Grange, to his. It was the way they wanted it.

Killiney to Sandycove

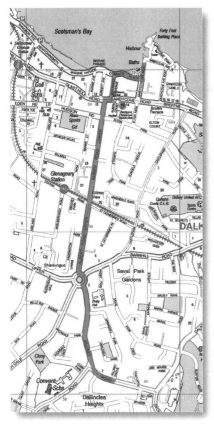

MY OLDER SISTER AND I would walk from Killiney down to nursery school in Sandycove. We were seven and five, that sort of age. My father did have a car, because he was a commercial traveller, but he was away during the week and my mother went around on a bicycle. There was a bus, and sometimes we'd get that, but most days we walked. Walking saved the few pennies for sweets. There was very little money around. My mother cut up squares of newspaper for lavatory paper. Though of course if she hadn't had a maid I suppose things would've been a lot easier.

Off we'd set. Turn sharp left at the gate. The neighbouring house was *Longleat*. I know now that it had been called after the English stately home. Because? The owner had been a gardener there before coming to Ireland. And brought the name with him. Pity that he didn't also bring a few lions. But he did obviously arrive with spades and rakes and horticultural equipment. Always were nice gardens around that house. History of the origin of house names is a study in itself.

In the 1950's there were actually very few houses on this part of Killiney Road. After Longleat and The Maples there was nothing. Fields and ponds and trees to the left, and *Urney* on the right, home of J.J.Kelly. Rumour had it that JJ had been a German spy in the war. But I remember him as a genial old buffer cutting his hedge. Though in later years he did wear a saffron kilt. Blokes in saffron kilts could be up to anything.

Opposite his house was the triangle. In those days it wasn't derelict and had a neat railing all the way around. Though kids would squeeze through to investigate. It was the septic tank for *Urney*. Septic tanks are very interesting. There was also the horse trough. Erected by horse philanthropists in Victorian times. And it still had water in it then, rather than geraniums, though I never saw a horse drinking there. Next house down was *Anglesea*. And from then on down it was just fields on both sides of the road.

In later years the fields to the left were filled with bungalows, and one of these was *Fairy Hill*.

My aunt lived there. Her name was Doris but they called her Dodie. She'd been a chorus girl. Her brother was a bookie. He wore yellow waistcoats. Not only was Dodie my aunt, she was my Godmother. We got on very well. She had no children of her own. But at one stage she did foster my two girl cousins from England, children of the more dysfunctional branch of the family. The girls lived here for years but then suddenly vanished. I was almost an adult before I heard what happened. They'd been taken away back to their slum in England, a move orchestrated as part of a family plan to get the girls' dysfunctional parents eligible for council housing. Oh yes we're cute enough, genetically speaking.

The older girl Maureen and I were very close in England in later years. Probably too close for first cousins. We had a love affair. But she died of the drink. And her sister vanished, forgotten by the family. A few years back I tracked her down. Working class, with a different name, in South London. A long way from the south side of Dublin and Killiney Road. She was really nice, wrote poetry. Herself and her husband came to visit in Ireland. She told me to always call her by the name she had been known in Ireland as a child. So I did. But then she too died, in her forties, of cancer. Her ashes are now in Dún Laoghaire. In my sister's flat. Waiting. There's an ongoing argument about where to bury them. Some elements of the family want them buried one place, other elements another. We're a fractious bunch. Unhappy fate, those girls. Shunted around as children, and unwanted ashes dead.

Further down on the right the local big house was *Proby Lodge*. Occupied when I was a child by a Major Anbespin. The genealogist in me wonders about that name, but reaches no conclusions. This part of Killiney Road actually runs through the grounds of *Proby Lodge*, and the little house on the left at the bottom, *Proby Cottage*, that was the gate lodge. South County Dublin is liberally sprinkled with Proby placenames. Not surprising, much of the land once formed part of the Proby Estate. All that started in the eighteenth century with John Proby of Huntingdonshire. He, wisely enough I suppose, married Elizabeth Allen, daughter of Viscount Allen of Stillorgan. The Allens had been a Dublin building family in the times of Charles 1. I've no idea what the daughter looked like but it didn't really matter. Marrying her was like marrying the daughter of an O'Reilly, or a Smurfit. But before the recession. Because Liz's Dad was the original owners of all these lands. Well, not the original, those were native Irish. But let's not go into that, we're all Europeans now. Things went from good to better for John Proby. He was shortly elevated to the peerage, becoming the first Lord Carysfort. And that's another name that crops up a lot in these parts. And OK, that's enough from the inner genealogist.

When Proby Lodge was demolished they built an apartment block there. And my great uncle's stepdaughter moved into one of the apartments. She was Pan Collins of RTÉ, Gay Byrne's sidekick on the Late Late Show. I visited her when I was writing the history of my family. She was very elderly then. But careful. And stayed pretty schtum about the more grisly details.

The roundabout at the bottom of Killiney Road was a simple crossroads up to thirty years ago. Not quite a country crossroads, maidens dancing and all that, but still reasonably rural. There was a ruin of a house on one side, *Avondale Hall*. As teenagers we played there. The tiled floors of the roofless kitchens were patches in the fields. The long gone house gives its name to the area, its own name deriving from the Parnell estate in Wicklow. Because? *Avondale Hall* was the home of Parnell's sisters.

The house *Rosney* was always there at the crossroads. And still is at the roundabout. In my childhood this was home of T.P.Robinson. A large solicitors' practice of that name survives in Dublin. As indeed does TP's son, Harry. President of Killiney Golf Club in his time. That sort of house, that sort of family. But times change. It's now the home of a journalist, Bruce Arnold. My inner historian knows *Rosney* as an 1830's villa, onetime home of people called Waldron, wealthy fabric printers from Rathgar. Book learning. But it was not until twenty five years after childhood that I first went through the gates. To have a shouting match with the aforementioned Bruce and his good lady Mavis. Another story, later, later.

Albert Road itself has always been there, always built up in my lifetime anyway. And looks very much the same. The upper half is lined with very bungalow sort of bungalows. Complete with verandahs. Actually very nice and if I'd spent a lifetime working in India I'd have retired into one of these, no bother. Architecturally speaking we have a definite touch of the Raj here, and why not? After all the road is called after Prince Albert, consort of the Empress of India.

For reasons connected to the 59 bus, my sister and I always walked home from nursery school up the left hand side of the road. That way, if tired, we could run to a bus stop and make the rest of the journey in comfort. If we hadn't spent our bus fare at the bottom of course. So we walked left hand side coming up. Rain, hail, or snow. We were tough kids, grew up hardy. I write, she married an academic. Both roles need a certain iron in the soul.

The left hand side of a road coming up is, of course, the right hand side going down. And walking up or down on Albert Road I always use that side. The habit has just stayed with me. To the extent that there would be something unnatural about walking on the other side. Much like which side of a bed a person likes to sleep in. Though I suppose that latter is complicated for people by the location of magnetic north and one's personal aura. And whether or not one has prostate trouble.

No I don't. The quip just came to me. Anyway, onward down the right hand side of the road. There is actually a stream here, running along beside the footpath, just over the garden walls. In the great majority of gardens this is now culverted over, but it is still there, as shopkeepers down in Glasthule find out when they get flooded in heavy rains. Those hidden streams are fascinating. Six hundred of them in Dublin, so they say. The web of them, beneath the layout of our own times. As if we live on a carpet of maps, layers of maps, one laid over the other and back to times unknown. Fascinating. But perhaps something Glasthule shopkeepers find less so when they're up to their knees in floodwater.

Glasthule itself in fact takes its name from one of these hidden streams. No, the placename has nothing to do with the surname 'Toole'. Trust me, I'm a gentleman and scholar. The former because I was born in Killiney and the second because I went to UCD…briefly. Glasthule takes its name from the Irish 'Stream of the Black Foreigners'. Seems that even then we were racists. Those particular black immigrant guys were Vikings. From Denmark. As distinct from Vikings from Norway. One crowd dark, the other blonde. Not that it made much difference if they were raping and pillaging you I suppose.

And there goes my invite to Scandinavian embassies.

Haddington Park on the left was home of my onetime friend Brian Ennis. Onetime, and longtime. He actually went to nursery school with me. A chemist in Dún Laoghaire still bears his father's name. Top of Marine Road. I last spoke to Brian at the bottom of another road. Merrion Avenue. It was midnight, or thereabouts. Driving out from Dublin, I was stopped by the lights. A figure lepped from the sidewalk. Opened the car door. Looked in. And said "oh it's you, good."

"Why good?" I asked, carefully.

He got into the car.

"Because you can take me to Stillorgan".

"I'm not going to Stillorgan".

"Take me to Stillorgan you bastard".

"Get out of my fucking car Brian".

He got out, but waved his finger silently and menacingly, as if to imply some awful fate in store. That was the end of our friendship. He didn't speak to me again. Shortly before he died, yes he died quite young of cancer, he walked past me in Glasthule, blanked me completely. Obviously he was, like myself, a man who bore a grudge. Or a man once very good looking and handsome, dashing even, a man who didn't want to talk to old friends with cancer written on his face. Perhaps a bit of both. Brian's widow Barbara is now headmistress of Rathdown School. I've never met her but I know the school is lucky with that leader. He was extraordinary. A one off. Wild and Byronic. He wore a cloak sometimes. And if she married him, there's a vision in her.

Life's journey continues. As does our walk down Albert Road. Now going past the graffitti sprayed shutters of the one time shops at the bridge. What would Mr O'Rourke think, I wonder. And his father in law before him who owned the shop when I was a child. And wore a brown shop coat like Ronnie Barker in TV's *Open All Hours*. All dead now. John O'Rourke married Catherine, daughter of that original owner. A commercial traveller, he met her in his business. And, as they say, he married into the place. Their whole story in this building. And no mourners for them here, or memories of their life's work. Their days of opening up, and closing down, and totting up the till. No memories now. Just the spoor of incoherent youths with spray cans. And property owners who couldn't be arsed about the look of their place.

Moving briskly along from that libel action. Number fifty two was home of my mate Ollie Macdonald. Or 'Colonel' as they call him in the Irish Army. His father was a mad barrister, if that's not tautological. Excavated a huge pit in the back garden. For no reason other than the digging. And almost opposite was the home of my mother's friend Moira O'Leary. I wrote about her recently in my *Irish Times* column. Google will reveal all. Move on. This is the internet age. Look it up if you want.

A new crossroads now. Hudson Road to the left, called after Joseph

'Sonny' Hudson. IRA hitman in the old days. His nephew is the Reverend Chris Hudson, Unitarian pastor in Belfast. One of the founders of the *Peace Train* movement, and an MBE. A fellow Dún Laoghaire citizen, and one of the guys around the place growing up. He and I were founders of the *New Ireland Arts Lab*. Nous? Pretentious? As Miss Piggy used to say. We used run big concerts in Blackrock Park. And Chris who was only Christy then wrote plays. They had to be seen to be believed. I interviewed him recently for an article. He'd found a different God than I. But I'm glad he found one anyway. He's been looking all his life.

Fitzgerald's was the 59 bus stop. Dr Cantan our doctor was in the house opposite when we were children. Dr Webb took over the practice from him. And as an adult I sort of went with the practice. As a patient. I suppose I could be described as an asset of the practice. Not a great asset really. Paying doctors' bills tends not to be a very high priority with me. "I know what's wrong with you as soon as you come through that door", old Webb said to me once. He didn't. What was wrong with me had nothing to do with doctoring.

If…if my sister and I hadn't spent our bus fare we might wait outside Fitzgerald's for the bus. If we had spent it we would have spent it in Gasparro's across the road. Now (yet another) wine shop. This is wine country we're in now. It certainly wasn't then. There were hens pecking round the junction. They came out of an alleyway beside Buckley's bookshop. Down that alleyway was the original Buckley's Auction Rooms. Old John Buckley. From Kerry. Not the presentday one, an earlier generation. You'd count your fingers after shaking hands with him. Of course you'd count your fingers after shaking hands with most Kerrymen. They just cannot be trusted. Something to do with geography I suppose.

Gasparro's was kid heaven. And Mrs G who ran the shop was something else. I maintain a picture in my mind of a very heavily made up lady. Beautifully turned out, as the saying has it. With a helmet of bouffant hair. And very friendly to the kids. But I suspect with adults different. Don't know why, some remembered childish instinct allied to grown up novelist's understanding, but I suspect she was a bit of a battleaxe. Her husband was a postman. Survived her death by decades. Love story? I think so. Something alone in his demeanour as he wandered alone around the borough. A small sunburned man, with spindly legs in shorts. I see their lovemaking, long ago before I was born.

9

The route to Sandycove, Sandycove Avenue West, yes that's where we're going, now takes us down Ballygihen Avenue. Or Ballygihan Avenue. The street names spell the word differently at either end. I prefer the Ballygihen myself. All these little roads linking the main route to the sea road were formerly the avenues to grand houses now mostly departed. Ballygihen Avenue was the home of the Glenavy family. The house at the bottom on the right. Lord Glenavy was James Campbell, noted Irish lawyer. He died in 1931. If you were born in the year he died you'd be seventy eight years old now. So it doesn't really matter, you're much the same as him.

Lady Beatrice of that ilk was a noted writer, as indeed was her son, Patrick Campbell. A humourist, he traded on his stutter. But anyone who remembers any of these people now is reading these pages through very thick glasses. Fame is fleeting. Campbell is history. Another humourist Hugh Leonard is only dead a few months as I write. I think he's forgotten already. And I was at the doctor's yesterday. He's put me on pills. The smallprint says that in rare cases they can give hallucinations. I've just taken the first. And I'm already seeing in my mind a little stone archway at the top of Ballygihen Avenue.

That stone archway is all that remains of the entrance to Ballygihen. As a very small child I liked it a lot. An imaginary castle. And as a teenager it was useful for pissing behind when thrown out of Fitzgeralds. And also for kissing girls. Though it wouldn't really be a very long embrace. Girls, who are sensitive, would tend to say Jesus this place stinks of piss. And insist on wriggling away. Though maybe they were just using that as an excuse. To wriggle away. I seem to recall lots of girls wriggling away even in the most sweet smelling of locations. Women. Anyway, that there is a multipurpose archway, with many histories unknowable and strange.

Last lap now.

Along the seafront. With multiplechoice options. As kids we could duck down the little stairs in the wall and make our way along that path...it's actually the roof of a gigantic sewer pipe bringing shit from Dalkey...yes there's a joke there somewhere, but I'm in a hurry now to get to school. Alternatively we could keep going on the footpath and through the shrubberies. Or, thirdly, we could take the route we were supposed to take. Told to take. Strictly instructed to take by our mother. Keep going on the footpath around the corner, avoiding the shrubbery. Because there's *men* in there. My mother had a certain way of saying the word *men*. Her tone actually didn't vary that much whether she was pointing out paedophiles in shrubberies or just men in the generality. Of course she did have six children.

'He gazed southward over the bay, empty save for the smokeplume of the mailboat vague on the bright skyline, and a sail tacking by the Muglins'.

And so it quotes on one of these stone memorials that seem to proliferate here. Joyce, Ulysses. Nicely put, Jim. But quotations from Joyce in public places always remind me of those shamrock signs they used put up outside Bord Failte approved B and B's. Quotations from Joyce are in fact the literary equivalent of a shamrock. God we're a desperate people. And this one in Sandycove is not at all helped by the fact that you can't see the bloody Muglins from here. More interesting and relevant to the world I know is the memorial to Denis Burton.

In later years, as in later pages we shall see, I was to live in this area. And Denis was my postman then. A very nice guy. Though some of the letters he brought me left a lot to be desired. Yes he did have that slight eccentricity, that difference, that vaguely off-the-wall personality that is common to all postmen. But he was a good bloke. I have lived in several countries. Take it from me. All postmen everwhere are, essentially, a little mad. The same with dentists. Only more so. All dentists are completely mad.

I have never met a sane dentist.

THE RESIDENTS REMEMBER OUR POSTMAN AND FRIEND
DENIS BURTON
1947 - 1996

13 SANDYCOVE AVENUE WEST

MISS MURRAY LIVED in this house with her brother Kevin. A bachelor, he was a railway enthusiast. And in fact wrote the history of the *Great Southern and Western Railway*. A portly and lugubrious man. She was small and energetic. And ran a nursery school. This consisted of one enormous table which the kids sat round with copybooks. In the corner there was a largish religious construction, an ersatz altar affair, almost big enough to say Mass. I now realise that Miss Murray's school had a lot in common with those Islamic madrassa institutions. We learnt by rote. We prayed in that corner a lot. We went out the door and off to St Joseph's in Glasthule… a lot. I remember that. Forgotten most everything else. Though I can still do mental arithmetic. And I do have beautiful handwriting.

Yes, most of my memories of the place are of going out that door and off to St Joseph's. Marching in a long crocodile to practice and rehearse for various liturgical functions. Including our First Communions, which we 'did'. That event itself I cannot actually recall. But I do have the medal somewhere. Not sure if I ever did get any Holy Communion money to 'still have', as the saying goes. But if I did, I don't. Instead I have stored away the memories. Clattering down the stairs, and the marching off towards the esplanade. And looking at the cormorants on the brown rocks of Scotsman's Bay. They're a sinister bird. They never seem to make a sound but if they did I'm sure you'd hear John Waters.

They say that Scotsman's Bay takes its name from ships that used to anchor there. Scotsmen. I dunno about that. Have written lots of local history books myself and don't trust the genre. Inaccurate waffle tends to get recycled. No matter. As little children we marched bravely along by that bay, no matter whence its name. Miss Murray led the way, her acolyte and assistant Patricia brought up the rear. We climbed on walls and messed around on the piano. Which of course is not a piano, but rather the memorial celebrating the start of construction of Marine Parade. It's just that people called it the piano. Started in 1922, that esplanade wasn't finished when I was a kid, and still isn't finished now in 2009. Though it does have one of the silliest sculptures this side of wherever silly sculptures gather. Called *Archer 2*, it's nonsense. But this is a world of nonsense, and I suppose it always was. The human condition.

Miss Murray, she is an enigma. It's hard to see her in my mind as other than a name. As a young girl watching her own breasts grow, and as an old woman wondering why no man crushed them in his hands. She is just a name. Murray. Miss. I'm not at all sure where those Murrays of Sandycove came from. Archbishop Murray from Arklow built the Pro Cathedral in Dublin. Maybe there's a connection there. The religious intensity would imply it anyway. And maybe the school had a connection to the Murrays who were next door neighbours but one. At number 11 Sandycove Avenue West. About them I know a lot. Because I noted them on the 1911 Census. An excellent online resource. Organised and paid for by Canadian interests. Thanks Canada. Yep, next door but one was Hugh Charles Murray. Born in County Cork in 1862, he was Registrar of the *Great Northern Railway Company*. And that rings a bell. A bell whose ringing echoes the railway interests of the school marm's brother. Us genealogists don't miss things like that. Hugh's wife was Josephine, who had been born in County Kildare. She was twelve years younger. Hugh had married her when she was around eighteen. And got down to the business of building a family. They already had nine children with them in the house in 1911. There was Cyril, a medical student, aged 18. He was followed by Hugh (15), May (13), Gladys (11), Desmond (8), the twins Pierre and Paul (5), Nives (2), and baby Michael, aged nought. Amazing. Good on you, Josephine from Kildare. But where the kids all fitted is none too clear. And they also had to make room for one Jeremiah O'Connor, the lodger. He was a 47 year old Civil Servant, and a widower.

I wondered if he fathered some of those children? I hear creaking on the stairs. I've a terrible mind. And the tension in that house worries me from down the years. That house  where there was also space for the maid, May Casey. Aged 24, she had been born in Birkenhead in Liverpool. Did the father of the house or the lodger give her one, to the sound of the lighthouse moaning in the fog at the end of the East Pier? And the smell of the sea like a perfume. How did her thighs feel to whatever man crept through her door? Probably much like the thighs of a girl today. That is a truth, planned in eternity. But that is a truth for a man, planned in eternity. But what is the truth for a woman, a truth planned in eternity? Who did that girl talk to, when she missed her period? That is a deeper truth. I worry about her loneliness. And apart from that I have absolutely no idea about anything.

No, I know nothing about the lives lived in Sandycove Avenue West a hundred years ago. And I seem to know even less about the modern day residents. Though I do know the solicitor Johnny Hooper lives down there on the corner. When I was a kid I admired him. Well he wasn't a solicitor then. I don't admire solicitors. I admired him because I was a little bugger interested in boats and he was one of the grown up big guys, Olympic yachtsman and all that. He married Gigi. Well I'm not sure that's her precise name. But she was a hairdresser. Called herself Gigi. And wasn't she a friend of Jackie, another hairdresser, from Sallynoggin? And wasn't Jackie a girlfriend of Freddie Cooney, who has *Knobs and Knockers* in Nassau Street? My God it's all coming back to me. But only in the vaguest way. I seem to know more about the folks of a hundred years ago. The thighs of long dead serving girls. I know them in a deeper sort of way. But then, I'm a genealogist. I like the long gone dead. I'm comfortable with them. And the mystery of it all. How their descendants rub our shoulders on the DART. Or sit in Auckland or Chicago, wondering about their roots. It's all about wondering really. Wondering in a sort of vacuum. Which glam hairdresser married whom is merely tittle tattle really. Though that Jackie one from the noggin was gorgeous. I can see her sultry eyes looking out from these words. Though that may be more hallucinations from the new pills. Whatever. The real long gone past is probably more significant than any of that, as is the unknown future. One wonders particularly about the future, and the chroniclers of one hundred years from now. What will they have to record? Perhaps not that much, because if things go as pear shaped as global warming theorists predict…well… this area will actually all be under water.

Time for prayer, methinks. Nearest church, Glasthule.

In the summer of 2008…which sounds like the start of a country song…but I can't help that…in the summer of 2008 I was doing a column for *The Irish Catholic* newspaper. Yes, summer. Because in media terms I'm very B List, the print equivalent of those poor failed schmucks who stand in for Pat Kenny and other holidaying RTÉ stars. I may even be C. But all that is only relevant to my personal sense of bitterness and regret. The point is, one of my pieces in *The Irish Catholic* was about this church. An outraged parishioner got on to the editor and denounced me for 'rambling on'. Which I took in the same spirit that the noted late writer J.G.Ballard adopted when accused of being 'beyond psychiatric help'. That is, mightily pleased. The Irish and Catholic editor agreed with my position and told me to keep rambling on. So here goes again.

St Joseph's is a very nice church. And should be. Designed by Edward Pugin and George Ashlin, an excellent design team who were responsible for scores of churches in their times. Pugin was English, and Ashlin, who was in fact his brother-in-law, was from Cork. If your business partner is sleeping with your sister it either goes one way or the other. In the Pugin/Ashlin scenario it went well. Pugin was son of the better known English architect Augustus Welby Pugin, assistant to Barry, the architect of the rebuilding of the Palace of Westminster. Augustus Pugin himself designed Maynooth College. The son had then taken on the practice when his father 'suffered mental collapse' and died at a very young age. Well that's what it says in his obituaries. Not sure how one can die of 'mental collapse'. I'm still here.

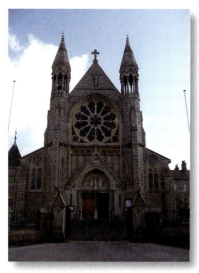

Built in 1869, St Joseph's nonetheless remains unfinished. To the right of the façade there was intended a whacking great spire in the French Gothic style. (Yes I know this stuff. Long before I was a writer I was in the architectural game). A pity about the missing spire, but I suppose they ran out of money. Maybe now is the time to get going on it?

Yes, the more I think of it! Hard economic times are surely best overcome by embarking on great spiritual adventures. There'd be no Chartres if the money had been spent instead on paying civil servants to sit on their arses doing bug all but wait for pensions. We (humans generally, and not just writers rambling on) suffer from varying hungers. And the fact and existence of Chartres is a meal in itself. Certainly if the state commenced the immediate building of Glasthule Spire it would take many people's minds off their mortgages.

I like Glasthule. Sort of. As a child Dalkey was our

**Bóthar Glas Túatail
GLASTHULE ROAD**

town and Dún Laoghaire was our city... but Glasthule was our village. The locations were distinct entities, and we did different things in each. We shopped in Dalkey, for food and such. And shopped in Dún Laoghaire for clothes and practical things like buckets. In Glasthule mainly as boys we just tried to avoid getting mugged. It was pretty much a noisome ghetto, and had been so for quite some years. In the late 1800's people had finally noticed the problems, and attempts were made to ameliorate conditions. The first artisan dwellings in the whole of Dún Laoghaire area were erected off Eden Road in 1896, and the little streets up there bear the names of prominent citizens of those times. Glasthule Buildings itself followed on in 1908. However this was a sort of early Ballymun, *ie* an architectural/social disaster, and was already a slum in the fifties. One of my mother's maids was raped on the walkway in the Buildings. But my mother said she wasn't the full shilling anyway. Not sure how that attitude would go down in the Rape Crisis Centre these days. But those were different times. And my mother was not politically correct. That same maid had a child as a result of the rape. And thirty years later I would see the two of them, ex-maid and daughter wandering round the town. The daughter had taken after the mother and neither of them were the full shilling. I would look at them and think it's terrible knowing too much about people. And wish I didn't know anything about anyone.

After nursery school I was sent to school in Dublin. St Conleth's. Can't you tell by my grammar? I'd come home on the bus and wait at this bus stop for the 59. Too old for walking up Albert Road by that stage. Aged about 10 or 11 I was mugged right here. My bus fare vanished with a gang of older gurriers across the car park and up into Eden Road. Bit archaic these days, that word, gurriers. But it can't really now be modernised as skangers or some such. Gurriers merely thumped their victims, rather than stab them or jump up and down on their heads. But robbed I was anyway. So I walked home. Bitter. And sometimes even now I look carefully at elderly faces in the bar of the Eagle House, trying to identify the culprits. Bitterly.

Six or seven years after that the boot was on the other foot. It was I that was the miscreant, and got myself arrested by a Glasthule cop. It was, of course, all the fault of women. Simple enough story. Myself and another teenager had girlfriends up in Rathdown School. They were boarders. So we went up to see them one night. As. One. Does. And were caught. My father gave me hell. But my mother reminded him of how he had himself been arrested at the same age for breaking the street lights in Blackrock. And my father was a friend of Dinny Whelan, the Glasthule garda who arrested me. His wife ran one of the shops in the village. Very different shops then. Cavistons was a humble fishmongers, very far from the foodie heaven of our times. And beside it was Smiths vegetable shop, run by a one armed man. He fascinated me as a child. How he could fill a sack of potatoes with one hand. A sight worth watching. The nephews of that man are the Smiths, who work as hauliers for Buckleys Auction Rooms. Yes it does, it does all hang together.

So that was that, the case of *Dinny Whelan versus Myself* was dropped. Much like myself by that same Rathdown girlfriend a few years later. I'd sort of kept her on, as backup to Charlotte, a working class girl I'd picked up at the funfair in Dún Laoghaire. Charlotte and me used make out in the alleyway up along Presentation School to Eden Road. And she features in my novel *The Nottingham Road Hotel* which, if there is still a book industry then, will be published next year. The Rathdown girl didn't know about the Charlotte liason. The class structure being what it was. Different circles. But nonetheless she dropped me. Dropped me in a fairly dramatic fashion too. A gang of us, aged 18 or 19 by then, were up around Vico in the middle of the night. Drink was involved. I had a friend Dick. He turned out to be aptly named. Wandering around in the darkness I came across him and my Rathdown girl in flagrante in the back of a car. Bare female limbs sticking akimbo around the place like something in a cartoon. But hey, Judy…I forgive you. Though just in case you're wondering, no I did not call my daughter of the same name after you. Just took bloody good care to send her to Coláiste Íosagáin rather than Rathdown.

This then is the place I grew up in in the 1960's. Looks peaceful enough in these photos. Less crowded perhaps, certainly less traffic. But none of that mattered. To most of us, and indeed to a great number of Irish people generally, the most important element of the town was that shown here below. The boat. Practically everybody I grew up with went away on that boat. And most didn't come back. But that is not this story. And nor are the words on the past few pages. Merely trying to set the scene. This is a love story.

AFRICA... AND...

YES, YES. I know Africa is not on the southside. But my walk took me one day down to that boat in Dún Laoghaire. We called it the Mail Boat. Slightly later it became 'the ferry'. Whatever, it was a grim sort of travelling. Blokes off to building sites, and girls to god knows what. I was a bit of a poet then, and distinctly got the impression of a nation bleeding to death. Funnily enough, forty years later, I'm beginning to get the same feeling again.

After living in Africa for some years I returned to Europe with a South African girl. Worked and wandered in Scandinavia. But she left me in northern Sweden. No, she's not still there. Leonie went back to South Africa. And we were in touch decades later. I left Sweden. Decided to go to Spain. Handily enough I met a Danish girl on a train. Vibeke had the same plan. She and I and other disturbed victims of an unfeeling society which didn't care or understand lived in a cave on a beach outside Barcelona for six months or so. Franco was still in power. The Guardia Civil were not a touchy feely force. *El Honor es mi Divisa* and all that. A good night was when we weren't woken up by a machine gun poking into our ribs and some plastic hatted bogman, or whatever the Spanish equivalent of bogman, roaring at us. A good day was when we had enough money to get drunk. There were good nights and bad nights. Good days and bad days. Travel broadens the mind.

Mind broadened, I left all that behind me and went to England. Meteoric career in catering. Starting as a kitchen porter I rose in a few months to be supervisor of a staff canteen in a south coast holiday camp. One of my jobs was making sure that chalet girls were wearing clothes under their uniform. Because they weren't allowed into the staff canteen without clothes under their uniform. We were very strict indeed about this. Standards are standards. The girls were great, many living on the fringes of prostitution, but lovely. I often wonder and worry about where many of them ended up, but don't like to think about it. My novel *The Colour of Her Eyes* addresses some of those girls, some of those thoughts.

Yes I like women. I've always got on well with women. A facet of personality that soon brought me back to Sweden with a girl I met in Sussex on a bus. We were both in Bergman mode. Wearing black. Mired in gloom. Marianne brought me to meet her parents. It went well. Her mother (wearing black and mired in gloom) regularly cooked me meatballs. And I worked in their town for a while. But the girl and I ran out of interest, and I suppose the mother ran out of meatballs. And I went back to England. Alone. And broke. Then back to Ireland. And landed up back walking around the southside. Alone. And broke.

BAMBOO COFFEE BAR

YES IT LOOKS VERY LIKE an Indian restaurant now. It is. But back then in the late 1960's it was the Bamboo, general hangout for people who hung out. Dorothy ran it. With a rod of sarcasm. An older woman, she maintained a mild contempt for us customers. It was well deserved. She should've upped the mild a notch. The location is George's Street Dún Laoghaire, that long straight road originally built by the British Military to link up their Martello Towers' defence system. In all honesty there wouldn't be that much basic infrastructure in Ireland if it weren't for the British. They were good at that. Our talents lie elsewhere. It's just that no-one has ever found where precisely that elusive 'elsewhere' is. It lies like Tir na nÓg. In a haze. Just over the horizon. Always over the horizon.

This part of Dún Laoghaire is a bit of a mess now. Actually most of the place is a bit of a mess now. But I suppose we have to remember that one of the first local authority officials in Ireland to be forced out of office for rampant corruption was the then Dún Laoghaire planning officer. That Mr Gibbons is dead now, so stop reaching for your lawyers, you other lot. You are fine upstanding. Etc. Fact is, many people walking round Dún Laoghaire ask themselves, how on earth did anyone get planning permission for that? Or that? The answer is simple. Corruption. But then, was it not always so?

Yes. Near the Bamboo Coffee Bar/Indian Restaurant is the elegant People's Park. Designed by John Loftus Robinson. He did the Town Hall too. A good architect, but also a councillor. Gave himself the commissions more or less. Yes, John Loftus and his fellow councillors were a bunch of back scratching cronies, thick as thieves, milking the system for all it was worth. But the thing is, the People's Park and the Town Hall are both quite beautiful. Whereas the results of our modern corruption seem to be ugliness, squalor, economic decay, general decline, all that.

But enough about George's Street. And the grumpy thoughts of a middleaged man returning to his home town. There's better memories here. Opposite the onetime Bamboo was Murrays record store and disco establishment. That was handy. Opposite also was the Cozy Bar. And a little further down Walters Pub. They were even handier. The Cozy and Walters are still there, albeit mightily altered. Murrays record store and disco is now a funeral parlour. There may be a message in that transition.

Opposite the Bamboo also was the laneway known as Stoneview. And as I write these words in 2009 I read in my morning newspaper about the death of Edward Delaney, sculptor. He had a little foundry down that lane. And would be seen limping up and down, planning in his mind no doubt his famous Dublin statues. For Thomas Davis, and Wolfe Tone. A dark and brooding man, Delaney, then. But the photo in my morning paper shows an old man, grey. And if it weren't for memory there would be nothing left of him, in 1968.

One day in 1968 a beautiful schoolgirl entered the Bamboo. A bunch of older blokes were sitting round a table. *Older* then was people in their mid to later twenties. I was one of them. Recently back from those years of hard times in Africa and elsewhere, I was discussing philosophy and the world situation. The Bamboo was that sort of place. Bob Geldof was one of the coterie. He has since brought our Bamboo conversations to the world stage. The beautiful schoolgirl and her friend lurked around our table, throwing shapes. Very good shapes too. I looked up from discussion of philosophy and the world situation and told myself I will marry her, that schoolgirl there.

The one called Hilary Cox.

I did.

Who was she?

WHO WAS THIS GIRL he decided to marry, where did she come from?

And who would she become?

Men are easy enough to understand. Women are more difficult. They live in places between mystery and simplicity. And somewhere there in the middle is another place called truth. It's a complicated truth, that woman thing. And a man is only ever going to see the half of it. But not even that much on any one particular day. Or at a particular time in her life, or whatever age she is. No single day's snapshot reveals. In fact a day's glance can give completely the wrong impression. When I met the schoolgirl she was… well…she was a sexy schoolgirl. With big tits, throwing shapes, the way a sexy schoolgirl will. What does a guy know, what does he think? He doesn't. He doesn't know and he doesn't think anything really. Or if he does, it's not with the thinking part of his body that he's thinking. What does he know of this girl?

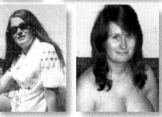

Nothing really. But he knows now.

She was the daughter of an Irish soldier. A soldier who had been killed while in the Irish army, doing whatever soldiers do. Not only that, she was the granddaughter of another soldier, a Dublin Fusilier. He had died at Ypres in the First World War. There was a pattern to that history. Just as her soldier father had been brought up by a widowed mother, she herself had been brought up by a widowed mother. And her mother's family came from republican people. They'd fought in the War of Independence, and in the Civil War. They'd gotten their reward.

Poor enough, they lived in a basement flat in Monkstown. It was damp and not that great. But they'd made the best of it. And there was a granny there too, and the granny too had her own story. Three generations of strong women. Cramped into a basement flat like they'd been collected. For some purpose, to illustrate, something. Not sure what that something is. But the pattern of the schoolgirl's history was of women, strong women. Doing what strong women do. Surviving.

A necessary skill that, particularly in Ireland. A country where the system does not give one bugger. And systems are, of course, made up of people. Those who wonder what caused the Famine have only got to look at the modern HSE. The lesson is there. Nothing to do with the horrible wicked Brits. It's all to do with ourselves. H's mother had been left with three children and a miniscule pension from the Army. Though they did also pay for the children's education. But H and her siblings learnt their major lesson elsewhere. God helps those who help themselves.

The bloke back from Africa looked at the girl. He didn't know any of that at the time, but that is what he recognised. And another thing. Even though she was very young, he saw another survivor in her. He had had his problems and his troubles. Done things and seen things best forgotten. And maybe she was too young to have had any real problems, real troubles. But he knew that when she did, when life came along the way it surely does, he knew that she would be tough and strong, and deal with them. He needed that. And there she was. But also of course there was the fact that she was gentle and beautiful. And moved through the scruffy coffee bar like she was music.

So he fell in love with her.

As mentioned.

This is a love story.

Bamboo Coffee Bar to Monkstown

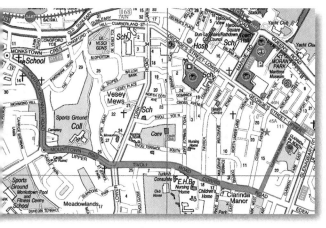

THE ROUTE from the Bamboo Coffee Bar to the altar in Monkstown Church took a few months. It meandered a bit. Perhaps she's a little too young, people said. Others were more emphatic. Don't marry that woman, urged my best friend, you'll regret it to the end of your days. You're making a big big mistake. Of course he was homosexual and fancied me something rotten so I'm not sure how unbiased was his judgement. He never actually came to terms with the marriage. And threatened in later years to get me with an axe. Conscious of the fate of Joe Orton, I discontinued the friendship.

What am I saying? Who remembers Joe Orton now? Playwright? *Prick Up Your Ears*, all that? Done to death with an axe by his boyfriend? Nah, rings no bells these days. Whatever, it was a simple story. His jealous boyfriend axed him. Older, a failed writer, he was jealous of Orton's fame. But mostly of his talent. Talent annoys people who haven't got it. I know that. If I hadn't got talent it would annoy the hell out of me. Just as my talent annoys the hell out of other people. So perhaps it was that. Perhaps that's why my friend was heading towards me with the axe. Perhaps it had nothing to do with the woman I would marry. Hmmnn. Bottom line is though, it doesn't really make much difference for what specific reason a bloke buries an axe in your skull. Your brains on the ground are beyond analysing such matters.

Walk on.

The route from the Bamboo to Monkstown meanders. We take a sharp left coming out of the coffee bar. For a moment it is years ago. We go past the jewellers then owned by a man mysteriously known as *The Snake*. I have no idea why. And past the gents' outfitters known as *Frank Martin*. That shop is gone. But strange, not a few days before I write these words I had a meeting…well…a lunch with Niall Martin of RTÉ. In O'Rourkes of Blackrock. Niall is son of the same Frank, the *Clothes for*

The More Mature Man Frank. A producer in Montrose, Niall wants to make me famous. Discussions are ongoing. But I didn't get where I am today by earning big bucks in TV, so we'll just have to wait and see.

Opposite here is Alex's shop. No longer Alex personally, he's moved up to the corner of Clarinda Park. This original Alex used be the post office. Combined with a shoemakers. I knew the daughter of that shoemaker. I last saw her in Durban South Africa. Saw her by accident. We drank guava juice together. And discussed Dún Laoghaire like it was somewhere very far away. She's dead now. Was teenage girlfriend of a bloke who, in 2009, threw protesting eggs at the directors of a bank. Yes it all hangs together. But how come everyone I know dies so young? Lucky to make it to forty a lot of them.

But I go on.

Another left turn up into Clarinda Park. Developed in the 1850's, and shoddy enough spec housing, it had deteriorated into a warren of bedsitters and bullshit.

Cnoc na Carraige
CLARINDA PARK WEST

If I had a whatever for the number of times I've been in bedsitters in Clarinda Park talking bullshit then I'd be a far less wiser man. Leonard Cohen has a lot to answer for. And if I had a whatever for the number of girls I've been with in bedsitters in Clarinda Park…though come to think of it, some of those were in Crosthwaite Park. In bedsitters. Oh God, the memories. A nurse. A check out girl. A something else. Looking back they all seemed to have had identifiable sorts of jobs. Or is it just that I classify them like this, a sort of tick off list. Today a check out girl, tomorrow a neurosurgeon. Figure of speech…there were no neurosurgeons. Pity. Would be at the peak of her profession by now. And might come in handy if these pills don't work. But anyway, the schoolgirl I was to marry put a stop to all that. Most of it anyway. The bitch.

Long years ago my great grandfather Michael McGovern actually lived in Clarinda Park. But in a whole house. Number nine, north. From Drogheda, he was Managing Director of Todd Burns in Dublin's Mary Street. It's Penney's now. Fairly tragic history there. His daughter my grandmother Molly was in school in Belgium. Then Michael died suddenly, very young. There they go again. Dying young. The family fell into poverty. Molly was brought back from Belgium and sent to Eccles Street Convent. A looker with a look, she was one of those schoolgirls that gave lustful notions to Leopold Bloom. Hard luck to him because, having reached the age of consent, Molly was married off to a wealthy older man, my grandfather Alexander Conan. Arthur Conan Doyle's cousin. (I was determined to get that bit in. Every book I write I mention that family connection). And Michael's son Bob was given a job in Todd Byrnes. As a sort of substitute pension for his mother, my great grandmother Jane Carroll of Drogheda. Her cousins were in tobacco. Although she herself lived in poverty as a widow. In Haigh Terrace down the town. But maybe they sent her some Sweet Afton. But enough of that lot. I wrote a whole book about that family, *Grandfather's House*. Available in your local friendly bookshop.

Clarinda Park is built on lands once owned by George Smith, a wealthy quarryman and stone merchant. His day came when they decided to build Dún Laoghaire Harbour. Out of stone. In addition to that enterprise, he built several large houses in the locality. Out of stone. One of these survives here, Granite Hall. A bit grim looking. But maybe when it had a clear view of Dublin Bay it had a happier countenance. So on up and onto Corrig Road. This is actually the oldest road cutting through the Dún Laoghaire area. It extends to Dalkey, known as Carraig Road there, and back to Monkstown Castle, known as Tivoli Road in that direction. Built to link the mediaeval castles of Monkstown and Bulloch, it is likely to be following the route of a far earlier track. That track, going down to the sea at Dalkey, was an offshot of the Slí Cualann, the main artery from Dublin to the South East in ancient times. Right about here at the junction of Clarinda and Corrig there is a lost little village around an early Christian church. It was known as Kilnagashaugh. My book *Ancient Ireland* is widely available for those desperate for further information about these things. My best selling book *Ancient Ireland* in fact, selling thousands and thousands over the years. Though sales do seem to be tapering off. Maybe that says something about the times. Shortage of tourists? Or is interest in our past declining?

ÁRDÁN AN RÍ TOIR
ROYAL TERRACE EAST

Maybe. But not so fast as my interest in that paragraph. Onwards. We turn right and plod along. Long before I met the schoolgirl I would homeward plod this weary way, going back up to Killiney from Dún Laoghaire pubs late at night. Usually half cut. Sometimes alone, counting the steps between street lamps. Sometimes with a group of guys, talking about girls. Sometimes with an actual real live girl. Planning which exact gateway of which large darkly avenued house to lure her through. Working out at what point in the journey would such a move be appropriate. Courtship for teenagers back then was a complex and measured affair. More courtly, somehow. There were no mobile phones. Or email preliminaries. It was face to face, rather than facebook. The messages of hidden texts were not pre-presented there on screens. The subtexts were in gestures, smiles, and the touch of fingers. Time to hold her hand.

But that's all over for me now. I'm on my way from the Bamboo Coffee Bar to Monkstown to get married. No more gestures, smiles or tantalising touch of fingers. Get a grip man. Or, as my London daughter says, my daughter of the marriage that I'm going to, *get with the programme*. Further along here Corrig Road intersects with Corrig Avenue.

This would be confusing to tourists, if there were any tourists anymore. But the intersection simply arises because right about here was the big house Corrig Castle. And the avenue going down towards Dún Laoghaire centre was its avenue.

Tivoli Road. I know absolutely nothing about Tivoli Road. Except that there are nice georgian houses at the York Road end. And that my kinsman Arthur Perrin lived in Tivoli House in 1835. Before he built himself what is now Castle Park school in Dalkey. And that back along the road in that direction at the Eden Road railway bridge there is a single cottage. And that that survives from a row of cottages known as Perrin's Row. And I know that cottage was onetime home of the poet Padraic Colum. And later of the mother of the Dublin business bloke Gordon Colleary. Come to think, I know quite a lot about Tivoli Road.

Tivoli. The name reminds me of the amusement area in Copenhagen, Tivoli Gardens. My Danish friend Vibeke, I mentioned her earlier, she brought me there en route to Spain. For fun. She had just bought me a meal of wiener schnitzel. For nourishment. And we'd had a sexual encounter on the train during the night. For sex. Funnily enough the sex came first, then the meal, then the Tivoli Gardens. In Ireland I expect this would happen the other way around. But I suppose the Danes are different.

Vibeke paid for that meal because I was broke. A virtual hobo, which is a romantic term for bum. On my uppers. Thank God for Vibeke. But then, a man always meets a Vibeke when he needs one. She will never read this book. But I type my love and thanks into the page. And maybe it will get to her by some mysterious psychic path. To that place where kindred spirits gather. I can hear her giggle now as I reach York Road.

I know a lot about York Road. I wrote not long ago in *The Irish Times* about the Reverend Mr Harden who built up the St John's church there. But that's all online so I wont waste my space or readers' time. This is the age of the internet. Get with the programme.

Down Widow Gambles Hill. They say it's haunted. But show me a hill that isn't. Past the tennis club on the left, was never through those gates, riff raff to my class.

But John O'Shea of Goal comes to mind as I pass. For some reason I always associate him with that tennis club. And his wife in her little white tennis skirt hopping around Monkstown. And his twin sisters too. Older than myself and my circle, we only knew that lot by sight. And when one of the twins was killed in an accident abroad and the other came back we didn't know which one she was. My words a prayer for both.

Past Christian Brothers. My friend Niall Harkin was expelled from there for being a communist. Or because his mother Nora was a communist and a friend of Frank Ryan who fought in the Spanish Civil War. Or because Peadar O Donnell was her lodger. I never quite got the story right. But my friend Niall Harkin has repeated it frequently. And I get more confused all the time. But then he's a radical, my friend Niall. But later went on to become a teacher in Willow Park. Radical? Willow Park? I just don't get it, the paths of other's lives. Not a longtime friend, my friend Niall Harkin, not from way back when. But I'll keep him on. I've really only a couple of longtime friends. Of the male variety. Tend to fall out with men. Whereas women friends stay friends forever with me. Maybe I should've slept with the men friends. Might have hung on to them longer.

Past Hewett's Shop. The grandfather of that shop was a British Admiral, lived in Blackrock. Or so my father told me. Was a neighbour of his. And one of the sons of the admiral took to drink and ended up working in a filling station. As a small boy I was in my father's car when we found the son of the admiral filling us up with petrol. My father told me then. Let that be a lesson to you, he said. Admiral and petrol attendant. Decline and fall.

Carrickbrennan Road, a place of poetry, in a way. Meandering here I'm reminded that the schoolgirl I'm on my way to marry owns a book. A poetry book by Seamus Heaney. Inscribed to her in personal handwriting. *With thanks. For all your help. Seamus.* I'm reminded of that because the late Christopher Daybell lived right here on Carrickbrennan Road. Poets,

Heaney and Daybell both. And almighty bores with it. Daybell, being dead, is now marginally less boring but your other guy goes on and bloody on. 75 euros for his poetry CD? Are they barking mad? The man's a bore. Let's be honest for once. He bores the country stiff. But we're too bloody polite. Or insecure. None of our emperors have any bloody clothes. And anyway even if they insisted on doing it for his seventieth birthday, wouldn't it have been better to charge seventy euro, one euro for each boring year of his boring life? Somehow more marketable that way.

Christopher Daybell would have understood that. A self proclaimed poet of the people, a street creature, a bard, a wandering seller of photocopied sheets of verse, he spent his life sidling shiftily up to innocent foreign girls in Grafton Street and saying in that educated English accent, "do you read poetry?" He made a good living selling his doggerel. And what's more, even though he had no teeth, little hair and less talent, he seemed always to be swanning around with one or another bit of continental tottie on his arm. Then he married Symphorosa. So she became Symphorosa Daybell. Good name for a woman. The family house along here was *Dillychip*. Terrible name for a house.

The marriage did not last. The last time I saw him he was shuffling along here alone, in rag order. He died shortly afterwards. God it was all so hopeless. He was mad, really. But he's dead and in good company now, the ghosts of Carrickbrennan Road. There's lots of them. And another one of those ghosts was another friend. But a real friend, not a glorified acquaintance like ding dong Daybell.

The last time I saw my real friend was also here. David O'Hare, walking along late at night. He lived up Richmond Avenue way. I suppose he was coming from Goggins. It wasn't the coming and going to pubs that killed him, rather the time he spent in them. Behind him walked his wife Neasa. They walked some yards apart. I suspected or I felt that they'd had a row, there was something in their walking. So I didn't stop the car. Then a few weeks later Neasa phoned me in the middle of another night. To tell me that he had died. It was a very bad time in my own life, as we shall see, as we shall see.

Yes, Carrickbrennan Road is indeed a road of ghosts, but not only the ghosts that a modern man like me might know. It's an ancient way, much widened in recent years. Carrickbrennan appears to derive from the Irish for *The Rock Of Braon*. And he appears to have been an eleventh century ruler. I have no idea where exactly his rock was, enough to note that all of this was rocky countryside. I suspect and suggest that the actual rock was more likely the hill running from the present day castle up to York Road, and see in my mind a cliff of granite there. And old Braon on top, keeping an eye out. And well he might. It appears...lots of things in this era of history 'appear'...it's a useful way of hedging bets...it appears that the area was actually settled by monks in the ninth century, they fleeing from areas across the bay that were more vulnerable to Viking attack. These would have been Celtic monks, followers of St Mochanna. And that was what they called their church, which was situated at the site of the ancient graveyard. But the presentday ruins are not the ruins of St Mochanna. After the Norman invasion the Celtic church was usurped, and their monks thrown out by Anglo Norman Cistercians who were based at St Mary's Abbey in Dublin. Mary Street. Abbey Street.

The present ruins in the old graveyard date only from the 17th century. A mere tick of time in the times of Carrickbrennan Road. It was those Cistercians built the original Monkstown Castle, to protect their lands and interests in the area. They also built Bulloch Castle at Dalkey, and the Corrig Road we have travelled was their route between them. Well did they need the castles, this was on the fringes of dangerous territory. Byrnes and the like, up the Wickow Mountains. They're still there, those mountainy guys. Anyone who has watched a gaelic football match in west Wicklow will know all about their destructive potential.

The Cistercians in their turn were thrown out at the dissolution of the monasteries. And it then passed into the hands of a succession of generals, thugs, place seekers, mercenaries...and a protestant bishop. The Pakenhams, family of the English Lords Longford, not to mention of Lady Antonia Fraser, widow of Harold Pinter, they are descended from this bishop. The succession of generals and thugs etcetera greatly enlarged the original castle over the centuries, and it became quite huge, extending over a wide area. That visible today is more or less only the front porch, in suburban architectural terms. Those who watched carefully coming down Gambles Hill will have noticed, in the modern random rubble walls, a very large proportion of cut stone blocks. These are from the walls of the demolished castle buildings. If walls could talk, I think the expression has it...well if walls could talk around here they'd have an awful lot to say. And if this photo of myself just back from Africa would talk, well then it would tell you stories.

MONKSTOWN CHURCH

ST PATRICK'S CHURCH in Monkstown was built in 1864. Another church by Ashlin and Pugin, it is an exercise in what they call mid Victorian Gothic. Well actually not just 'they', I trained as an architect and I call it that too. But I like to wear my learning lightly. It is really actually a very fine church, and worth popping through door for. I took this photo myself. I'm not a great photographer.

Another fine building is the neighbour, the church of my half seperated brethern on the far side of the road. This is something else. But perhaps because of its dominant position on the Monkstown Road we have got too used to it to appreciate what it's all about. Designed by John Semple in the 1830's, it is allegedly based on the Alhambra in Granada. Having never seen the Alhambra in Granada I can't really say. My knowledge of Spain is a haze of alcohol, women, policemen, and selling blood in dingy clinics to survive. Never did the Alhambra bit. Haven't been in Spain since.

I use the term half seperated brethern because I am half prod, my father and his people being completely that, protestant. Very. No taint of Roman Catholicism in that family. Except for the marrying in of my mother of course. Researches into the father's lot have revealed absolutely nothing but Protestants, Church of Ireland mostly, with a few Presbyterians thrown in to add a bit of misery to the mix. On top of which, my great grandmother on my mother's side was also Protestant. And Scottish to boot. More misery. I have no photo of her in which she is not holding a bible. Firmly. She had the air and dress sense of Queen Victoria. But probably wasn't quite so much fun. Bottom line is perhaps that I am a lot more than half protestant. DNA wise. But a Roman Catholic by upbringing. Whatever. In sometime moods I am a Christian, but never of particular variety. My protestant father was confirmed in Monkstown Church of Ireland. And, across the road some fifty years later, I was married in its Roman Catholic neighbour.

AMERICA

WE LEFT IRELAND almost immediately. A few days after marrying we went to America. H had just turned nineteen, not long out of school. I had a Green Card and a job waiting. We went from Cobh by ship, the QE2. Sounds posh, but we were penniless. The night before the ship docked in New York we won the bingo game. That money paid our fare up to New England.

Although in my mid twenties, and back from those years of wandering in Africa and other places, I didn't really know that much. Not important stuff anyway. The schoolgirl bride taught me things worth knowing. I suppose the two of us grew up there in America, very far from Dublin's southside. We definitely grew together.

Here we sit in the kitchen of our apartment at 165 Williams Street in Glastonbury, Connecticut. Some house, that. If a bit *Nightmare on Elm Street*. Or *Edward Scissorshands*. Whatever. The *Psycho* school of architecture.

It was very hot in summers. Snow up to the armpits in winters. H worked in downtown Hartford in a department store, selling coats. I worked in construction. And at Christmas I worked nights in a different apartment store. Selling ties and shirts. It was the American way. We reckoned we'd get rich. And move to California. Better summers milder winters there.

Siobhán was our first baby. But she died and is buried in Hartford Connecticut. The photo here was taken shortly after the baby's death. H doesn't look her best. She really wasn't well. I reckoned she'd be better back home in Ireland. So we jacked things in. Went up to Montreal. And got a ship from there to Liverpool. And another one from there to Dublin City. Can't remember what the weather was. But I somehow feel it should have rained.

H and CK, and the Glastonbury Fife and Drum Corps.

3A BRIGHTON TERRACE, MONKSTOWN

WE WERE'NT IN A GREAT STATE when we came back from America. The death of the baby had affected us very badly. I suppose we reckoned we'd get over it. But we never really have. That wraith has been a constant shadow. But then there's only shadow where there's light. And anytime our marriage teetered…as marriages do…the spirit of that child in America has watched over us. She lives in eternity, and visits us from there. I reckon we have that link to things beyond. Need that.

Certainly needed something on returning to Ireland at that time. The country was in bits. Much like now, I suppose, but in a different way. Not really quite so bad. There was certainly craziness and worries, some kind of cultural meltdown. People of our generation had taken to drugs, alternative lifestyles. Several I had grown up with were already dead from drugs. But the country wasn't really in the same sort of bits as it is now. Now there is a grimness and a gloom, close to despair. It permeates. Part of a worldwide thing, and a worldwide thinking…well that didn't work, what now?

And what then? Simpler answer to that question. We had little money, no jobs, and nowhere to live. But, a lesson learned in America, when the going gets tough… the tough get going.

So we got going… down to the mother-in-law, and stayed with her. A long time widow, she didn't have much money. Yes the house itself looked grand. Problem is Emer Cox lived in the basement flat. Which was cramped and damp. And her own mother lived there too. It was here that only a few years before she had made the bride's dress, and put on the party afterwards, right through that door there. Look at the milkbottles. There's history. Not sure when this photo was taken, or by whom, or even why. Only thing is it wasn't around the time of the wedding. No milk involved in the bottles then. It was a pretty damn good party.

We slept in the room where H had been a child. Funny vibe that. Like sleeping with a little girl. Paedophile by proxy. I never really understand those guys, just can't see the attraction. I reckon the nearest I'm going to get to any understanding is remembering what it was like, sleeping with H in the room where she was once a little girl. Whatever. The living arrangements just couldn't last, and didn't. After a few months we bought a trailer, a mobile home. Thanks to my godfather.

John Conan had been a teacher in St Gerard's School in Bray. I went

to visit him to say hello on my return. That was a learning curve, an exercise in understanding. Truth is, my mother's family have been bonkers for generations. Though my father used put it harsher, nodding, there's bad blood there. Despite that, I liked my Uncle John. As a child I had appreciated the tattoo on his upper arm, and as an adult I queried him about our family history, genealogy. He knew a lot, and talked about the old people. Doubtless his siblings also knew a lot, but they seemed to stay schtum, either through discretion or disinterest.

Around the time I returned from America he had given up school-teaching, or it had given him up, and he had moved into horticulture. Managing a garden centre. And one of his apprentices was Dermot O'Neill, the onetime radio gardener. Can't say fairer than that. Though my father didn't say anything fairer at all about that side of the family. Just nodded, ominously.

Bad blood there.

Anyway, whatever about the bad bloodlines, John had recently been evicted and, at the time of my visit, was living in a mobile home plonked outside the repossessed house, right there on the green at Old Conna. There he was living with his wife and daughters. Mary was one of them. She is now Mary White, TD, Green Party. And Lucy too. She is now a producer in RTÉ. Which goes to show that eviction and a spell of caravan living never does anyone any harm. It's all about genetics. Yes, while some people brought up in caravans may end smashing up pubs and in slasher fights at weddings, others become Deputy Leader of the Green Party.

Inspired by this visit, H and I decided that this was the way to go. Though I think my inspiration may have been somewhat stronger than hers. But she had promised to love honour obey. Make her bed and lie on it. When H makes a bed she lies on it. Whereas I start brooding about the colour of the sheets. And soon after the visit the godfather got himself a better mobile home, and a field up the road behind Bray to put it in. The old one was for sale. We had still nowhere to live. So we bought it. Good move.

Well, bad move actually.

The plan had been to put it on a site and go all jumbalaya. Enjoy a little bit of American style trailer trash living. I was thinking chickens near the door. H in tight teeshirt. And the sound of Johnny Cash singing *Folsom Prison Blues*. But there were just no sites to park the trailer. None that I was going to have my beloved H living on anyway. Defeated, we brought it to Arklow and dumped it on a seaside holiday park. To await the next move. The next move was to a bedsitter in a Dún Laoghaire slum.

Brighton Terrace to Adelaide Street

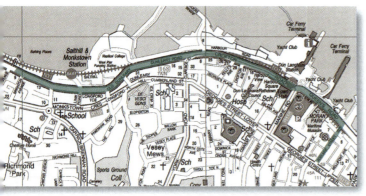

HARD TO IMAGINE NOW but, in 1807, two troopships were bashed up here on the rocks in a storm. Four hundred people were drowned, and the bodies are to be found buried in little graveyards along the coast. Some up in Carrickbrennan Road, and others in that graveyard on the Merrion Road. Behind the filling station. Turn left just before those bankrupt apartment blocks at Merrion Gates.

The loss of these troopships was, in 1807 terms, something along the equivalent of 9/11 in our own times. A shock to the system. However, since Iraq and Afghanistan were already invaded in 1807, more practical measures were taken by the authorities. They decided to build a harbour. A gigantic harbour. And there it is in front of us as we head towards Dún Laoghaire.

An elegant airy road, this stretch here. The parklands…linear park is the correct term…according to Dún Laoghaire Rathdown County Council …to our left are built on the onetime gardens of the fine big houses to the right. This road was private originally and, in fact, did not extend the whole way between Blackrock and Dún Laoghaire. It was only finally opened up to through traffic in the 1930's. That was a long time ago, not in my own time…when is a man's time 'his' time? Good question. No answer.

In my own time the Salthill Station carpark was site of the Longford Tennis Club. As a teenager I played tennis up in the posher Glenageary club but came down to Longford to look for girls at the dances. Don't think Glenageary did girls. Too posh. Myself and other testosterone fuelled gobdaws would descend half pissed on the ramshackle clubhouse that was here. Can't remember the girls but do remember the fights. Little did I know that the girl I was really looking for was only five hundred yards away in Brighton Terrace. Aged ten. Perhaps just as well that I didn't know that then. Or there I'd be, filed under 'K' on the sex register. Hate that.

I walk past Clifton Avenue and the shadow of a past time looms to my right. The shadow is myself, coming down there from Goggins with Madge. Taking her back to her flat in Clifton Terrace to shag her. But half way down the road she fell into a hole in some roadworks on the sidewalk. Drink? Involved. I hauled her out. Suddenly she looked very tousled and young and vulnerable. And I felt ashamed that I was taking her home to her flat to shag her. So I just took her back there and said goodnight on the doorstep. Kissed her and tidied her hair with my fingertips. There really wasn't much else I could tidy about her life. Yes it's a cop out. But I'm not the saviour of the world. Hard put to save myself.

She was lovely. Lovely and a raving alcoholic and held down a good job in publishing. And I know that they did their best for her at work. But, like me, there was nothing they could do to tidy her life. Madge is dead now. But if her shade comes across this here particular product of the Irish publishing industry, then she will know that it was her that set me off on my rocky path to feminism. Whether that's good or bad in the spirit world I do not know, but thank you anyway, ghostly Madge.

My footsteps count the years. Twenty years before the Madge-in-a-hole event I was also walking long here. Just back from America, taking another young and vulnerable woman back to a slum in Adelaide Street. To shag her also I suppose. But strangely, with H I was always a bit of a feminist. She has always been a person first. Being the bird in the bed mere happenstance. Strange, that.

Opposite now the entrance gateways to the Salthill apartments, obviously salvaged from some disused church someplace. Someplace that I don't know. Should. I'm an architect and local historian and novelist and genealogist and all round pain in the arse know-all but I've never bothered to find out. There's a limit to my nerdiness on these things. The apartments themselves are built on the site of the onetime Salthill Hotel. Which, even in the mysterious 'my time', always seemed to be derelict. When it was about to be bulldozed we…we being myself and certain dodgy associates in the architectural salvage business…scavengers…we went in and got loads of interesting Victorian items.

But (Judge) they were going to be bulldozed anyway.

How far I was above Essential Native Irish Knacker at this stage remains unclear. But needs must. We sold most of the stuff but I kept some for the building of my house in Mayo. Thus it happens that, as I came down the stairs this morning to work, my beringed and aristocratic hand slid lighty over elegant bannisters…elegant bannisters that once graced the Salthill Hotel.

Moving along. On our right hand side now is Longford Terrace. This is one of the great planned terraces of the onetime 'Kingstown'. In decline up to quite recent years, the houses were mostly broken up into flats and bedsitters, occupied by a mixture of decayed gentry and riff raff of varying factions. My own Granny Kennedy lived here in her old age, she falling into the decayed gentry category. Strangely, fifty years before that, her husband, my grandfather, he had lived as a young man in number four. I suppose he fell into the riff raff faction in those times. Is there something sad about a young and raffish man living in a flat in his youth, and sixty or so years later his widow living in a similar flat a few doors down? Would the ghost of one not beckon to the other in some way?

No answers from the page, so onwards through old Dunleary. Birthplace of our town. A few buildings on a busy road now, but once a harbour village of some size. Its roots are ancient, and can still be heard, a few steps up the hill. There's a manhole there and the rushing sound of water, that is the sound of ancient times, the sound of the past. A hidden stream that comes down to the shoreline here, it runs hidden underground way from way up by Monkstown Castle and beyond. And holy hairy ragged men followed it inland to found their hermitages of prayer.

A fishing port, old Dunleary was also used by cross channel boats in the 17th and 18th centuries, when weather prevented them getting in to Ringsend. Edmund Ludlow the Cromwellian general left from here in 1655. After putting manners on the Irish. He's the one famous for describing the Burren in County Clare as "a country where there is not enough water to drown a man, wood enough to hang one, nor earth enough to bury him". Also Jonathan Swift records that he himself embarked from here. And how the locals tricked him by overcharging for the row out to the ship. The satirical dean attempted to revenge himself by recording for posterity the bad character of Dunleary boatmen. But few read Swift now, and the crime and its revenge are equally forgotten. It happens. We writers scribble and tap away in futile hopes. There is no eternity for our words, or who we were and what we thought, or where we went and who we loved. Bear that in mind, Colm Tóibín, and cheer up for christsakes.

There's new Old Dunleary and old Old Dunleary. This latter had a different pier, now buried beneath the modern pier. But new Old Dunleary pier survives as the pier to the inner harbour. It was built it the 1750's by one Captain Charles Vallancey. A forgotten name, but one can walk down his pier today. Stone is a good thing to invest one's time in. Certainly a better bet than words. Bear that in mind, Colm Tóibín. I'll lend you a chisel.

It was said in the past that Dunleary was a place for 'a cup of good ale', but that the visitor should bring their own 'meat and wine'. I suppose much the same could be said today, despite modern Dunleary being centred on *The Purty Kitchen* pub. In days I messed with boats a haunt of mine. But no longer after that. Never quite got it. Depressed me. Even more depressing in its revamped guise of brown bread and smoked salmon. And tourists nervously sipping Guinness, glasses, not pints. Worries me, all that.

Now here beside the railway line we are actually walking on water. Because this is a causeway built across the original Dún Laoghaire Harbour, located exactly where the apartment blocks to our right are built. There's bits of old ships in the sands beneath those apartments. Lobster pots and the like. And the ghosts of sailors and their whores. And up over there on the height was the dún…which means 'fort'…of Laoghaire. Yes…King Laoghaire had a fort up there and, with a bit of imagination, we can see him scanning the horizon for troublemakers. Not that there's much on the horizon these days. The harbour is in decline. That high speed ferry is only going through the motions. I suspect that by the time this book entrances the readers' eyes it will be no more. And there's really not much else, maritime traffic wise.

A man looks around. Behind the West Pier there was the sailing club where I leaned about boats. George Craig taught me to sail. He thought I was a hooligan. Didn't like my winklepickers. But he did teach me to sail. And had an elegant and rather attractive blonde wife. A sort of unattainable Mrs Robinson to us teenagers. She drowned herself in a suicide off the West Pier. As did a girl I knew. Margaret Whelan. Walked down the pier. Took off all her clothes, piled them neatly. And jumped in and drowned. I remember her singing at a party. She was pretty, and had a lovely voice. But I reckon it's hard to know about the music in a person's head.

That sailing club is long derelict now. And the slipway at the Coal Harbour where Jim Malcolm and I kept our rowing boat? Inaccessible. Hidden beneath the tarmac carpark. As indeed are the remains of several beautiful cut stone buildings. Ah hah, I do not forget. I am an architect, trust me. Those buildings had to be moved to build the ferryport. With great fanfare the harbour authorities dismantled them and carefully numbered the stones. For re-erection. They forgot. The stones are now the carpark's foundations.

It figures. The Dún Laoghaire Harbour Authority is a Zimbabwean style entity, made up of political placemen and the usual hacks. With very very bad taste. Look at that ugly signage everywhere. Ugly signage is always a sign of decay. The whole place is commercialised and privatised in a haphazard manner. The results? The granite unity of the harbour almost completely destroyed. For nothing. No commercial gain. It's bust and bankrupt. Marina my arse. The place is an ugly storage pond for disused plastic boats, waiting to be repossessed.

Do I go on? I go on.

 I go on past a fine terrace of five nice buildings, here to our right, Connaught Place. I have a certain affinity with this terrace. And when I am recalling travelling along here to live in a slum in Adelaide Street that affinity comes baggaged with a certain poignancy. Connaught Place was owned by my great grandfather Joseph Conan. All five houses, he was a wealthy man. But sadly between him and myself there was the intervention of a couple of extravagent generations. Though Joseph himself was careful enough, selling the terrace and building two large houses up on Monkstown's Knapton Road for his daughters. One of these he called Tulach, the other Ardán. That's the houses, not the daughters. They were Jeannie and Josie. Jeannie was in the Gaelic League, and she would have known quite well that Tulach means burial mound, and Ardán a high place in the sun.

These were very very strange people.

Thank God I turned out normal.

Going on, to the right now is the Magdalene Asylum and Refuge. Built in 1879, this was for destitutes and penitents. H and my second child Alex was born there. His parents were indeed fairly destitute at the time, but hadn't got round to the penitence bit. Of course by the time he was born it called itself St Michael's Nursing Home. Now an empty looking structure, I've no idea what's going on in there. It seems to be very like one of those assets of a bankrupt property developer. The deeds tied up in a bad bank somewhere. National Assets Management Agency.

Crofton Road was originally Board of Works road, and along here were the offices and depots and workshops associated with the harbour construction and activities. There was in fact a little mini harbour, known as the depot, across the railway and now buried under the ferry terminal. On the right here the large building was onetime mansion flats, full of strange forgotten survivors of old decency, widows and retired colonels from colonial services. The building was at that time owned by the Pratt family, who later went on to own the Avoca chain of upmarket souvenir shops. Now offices, I'm not at all sure what happened to the residents, the widows and colonels. Apart from death. The next building along was the onetime Anglesea Hotel. It also is now offices. An awful lot of offices around the place. One wonders. One wonders, and looks then to the left.

And to our left. The station.. 1837. John Skipton Mulvany. Don't skip that *skipton*, for some reason he's never mentioned without it. Great architect. Think Broadstone. And opposite we note the rebuilt Victoria Fountain. Old one was destroyed by provos in 1981. There's a blow for freedom. And to the right the Town Hall. 1878. John Loftus Robinson. Good workaday architect. He modelled the building on a Venetian palace, and it was admired by Ruskin. But then Ruskin did tend to admire stuff modelled on Venetian palaces. Difficult enough guy, I should imagine. They say he refused to consumate his marriage, for aesthetic reasons. Wife hopped it sharpish.

Bóthar Crofton
CROFTON ROAD

We're heading for Adelaide Street. Best thing to cross the road here and make along the metals. Carefully avoid and do not sit down at a single one of those pavement café tables. There's philosophers about. That long haired bloke sitting there in a seemingly mystic daze is John Waters, my fellow *Irish Times* columnist. Well, not 'fellow' anymore because I had to quit to write some books. Including this one. Let's hope the sacrifice is appreciated. Yes John Waters always seems to be hanging round here. Brooding, ominous. Watching, something like a cormorant on those rocks at Sandycove. Yes, a cormorant…but crossed with that raven in Edgar Allen Poe. Tapping. Watching.

So, avoid the tables of the coffee shops, there's little there but the foolish philosophies of bitter people. But take a pause to stand and look across the railway line at the Royal St George's Yacht Club. Built in 1866 (and also by Mulvany, John, Skipton), and thus an excellent building, but as uninteresting as any yacht club except for one detail of its history. After Mulvany's death there was an architectural competition concerned with developing the building, and Messrs Lanyon Lynn and Lanyon of Belfast won it. A distinguished crowd, they also designed St Andrews Church aka the Tourist Centre in Dublin. However a couple of the members, Mr Owen and Mr O'Kelly, subverted the competition and contrived to get the job for themselves. 'The more respectable and influential the body', a commentator of the time wrote, 'the more corporate delinquency we may expect'.

True for you, commentator of the time.

We move on. These metals were…as everyone knows, but I'll repeat it, which is what us writers of local history do, we repeat each other…the metals were the route of a mini railway system that brought stone down from the quarries to build the harbour. The later, proper railway was then built in cuttings alongside, following the metals' route towards Dalkey. And to Bray, Greystones, and more exotic places beyond. Arklow even.

Glance to our right at the multi storey car park of the shopping centre, up there on an eminence where once stood Gresham Terrace. Not the earliest, Sussex Parade in Marine Road has that honour, but Gresham was the finest and bestest of all Dún Laoghaire terraces. Built by he of the eponymous Dublin hotel, its rubble was dumped into the harbour in front of the George Yacht Club to make a place for parking boats. No, you couldn't make it up. Up on the right also, more positively, we will see the recently revamped Marine Hotel. Originally the Hayes Royal Hotel, and built in 1828, they do what the English call a clotted cream tea. Not quite as good as that available on what the English call the mainland, nonetheless a certain leading Irish writer has been known to drop in there of a Sunday afternoon. With one of his few remaining male friends, John Cully, an architect. After a stroll down the pier. In the lateish summers of their lives.

 Shortly after the hotel we will see the 1840 Mariners' Church. A maritime museum now, it always seems to be closed. I suspect we Irish aren't that interested in maritime affairs. Certainly if we had of been during the Famine we wouldn't have starved so much. What with the seas around us lepping with fish. Looming now over us is one of the great public sculptures of Ireland. It stands on a rocky outcrop, the remains of the onetime Churl Rocks which were here to menace sailors before the harbour came along. This is the statue of Christ the King, by the American-Irish Andrew O'Connor. I love this

sculpture. It is my David, my Pieta, even my Venus de Milo, all rolled into one. It beckons us to greater things. And yes of course we can ignore that beckoning but, once seen, we and our silly sins are in its shadow. So, come on sinners, let's walk on. But quickly note over the railway line the monument commemorating the foundation stone of the harbour. 1821. Thackeray noted it too. He said "on my arrival in Kingstown I was confronted by a hideous erection comprising of a crown atop four fat balls. Apparantly it's dedicated to George IV. And seems eminently appropropriate to that monarch".

Boom boom.

Not far past here we arrive at a steps up to our right. Up the steps and we are in Adelaide Street. And the street sign will confirm that fact thrice. Twice in English, and once in Irish. Well, sort of Irish.

Laid out in 1838, it takes its name from Princess Adelaide of Saxe Meiningen, Queen Consort of the United Kingdom's King William IV. His coronation had been in 1831, and I reckon the excitement of all that got the good citizens of Dublin even more patriotic than usual. The place is coming down with Adelaide this and Adelaide that. It must be noted though that history actually records her as a very nice person, a home body and a home maker, accepting old George's illegitimate offspring as her own, and being generally a good influence on her onetime wayward husband. Would that every man should have a wife like that.

Walk up the street a way and think of a pub in Foxford in County Mayo on the bridge over the mighty Moy. And why, why think that? No reason other than that once long years ago there was a young barman in this Kingston Hotel right here, and now he is Pat Guirey, and owns that pub in Foxford in County Mayo on the bridge over the mighty Moy. Such thoughts mark the passing of time. We call them memories, but they are actually little chuckles from life itself, life marking our cards.

Onward, another little way. We will note the elaborate stucco decorations which enrich the Victorian terraces. Well, enrich most of them. For some reason number 31 has no decorations whatsover, neither elaborate stucco nor anything at all. It is plain and coloured pink, that particular pink that used be mockingly assigned to nuns' knickers. An inappropriate colour, now that I think.

31 ADELAIDE STREET, DÚN LAOGHAIRE

MY GRANDFATHER FREDERICK KENNEDY had lived in Adelaide Street in Dún Laoghaire with his first wife Jeannette Butler. But I didn't know that when after the caravan debacle we set up home in the street. I didn't really know anything about my grandfather then. Except that he had been very rich. And that my father had been comparitively poor. Frederick and Jeannette had a daughter here in the street. At number nine. Frederick's wife died here, and he moved to Monkstown. And there the little girl Jeannette also died, aged 11. I didn't even know the child existed until I found her grave in Mount Jerome, a year or so back, when I was studying family history. Since then I have always thought of her as a small girl running about Adelaide Street. Ghostly, she has become a sort of shadow of my own daughter buried in America. I like to watch, that ghostly little girl, running around. She and my daughter seem to be the one now, and yes perhaps that's not fair on either. Because they are separate people really, separate ghosts. But they are my blood, my DNA. Which sort of makes them much the same. What do ghosts care about time or differences anyway, the whys or the whens or the ifs. There's no *if* in the spirit world. That's just our thing, human stuff. And if we had brought that little girl home she too would have been running round Adelaide Street. But we didn't. And she didn't. She stayed in Hartford, which is a long way away, hard to visit. So instead I visit little Jeannette in Harold's Cross. And bring flowers and that. She has no-one else. It's a tumbledown grave. I'm crazy I suppose. With sorrow.

Setting up home is a grand term. Our residence was a glorified bedsit in a building which was, essentially, as mentioned, a slum. I'm not sure what is the legal definition of a slum, but I suppose the landlord did. He was a lawyer. And, stereotype piled upon stereotype, he was a Jewish lawyer to boot. But what could he do? The country was, as mentioned, in bits. Looks like it may be much the same today. Apart from the introduction of wheelie bins, the street front of the house hadn't changed a bit when our photographer went round in May of '09. Same carefully stacked rubbish at the bottom of the steps, same horticultural approach. Nothing had changed. Has to be that way, I suppose, it's a conservation area.

We settled in. Upstairs lived David Bedlow. He worked for the Commissioners of Irish Lights. And played organ Sundays in Rathdown Church. On the top floor, naturally enough, lived one Dennis McCullagh and his wife Elma. At first we all had little dinner parties. Mateus Rosé could very well have been involved. But Dennis was headed to being a Senior Counsel, which he is now. And Elma was headed towards being wife of a judge, which she is not quite, yet. But maybe Dennis will still make it. I hope so. I like the wives of judges. But then, maybe I'm prejudiced in that because I know Nuala Johnson. From way back when. Wife of the recently retired President of the High Court. She's great. Her father was a paddy builder in London. Wimbledon. Arrived off the boat with a shovel and a pick. And look at Nuala Johnson now. But whatever. Back in Adelaide Street the McCullaghs and Bedlow were going in one direction in life, we another. Our paths diverged dramatically.

I suppose we were some class of hippies. A lot of people we knew were on drugs, or in need of psychiatric care. Or both. It was the seasons of those times. H and I ourselves were never into drugs. Apart maybe from an awful lot of alcohol. We certainly seemed to have spent a lot of time in the Carney Arms, now the Kingston Hotel just down the street. I knew Carney. He was a sportscar driving likely lad. And was killed in a car accident. One wonders how many people remember such a detail. Few enough.

In Adelaide Street there developed a certain amount of creativity in lifestyle and personal relationships. (Yes, I am a professional writer, and know how to phrase these things well). Those who know know, because the times belong to them. And those who don't know, well, it's none of their damn business really. Conscious that H is now a grandmother, and probably doesn't want her grandchildren reading about what the tabloids could very well describe as three in a bed sex romps in Dún Laoghaire's Adelaide Street, I would leave the matter there. But of course I can't. There'd be no point in writing about Adelaide Street if I left the matter there. Might as well drop the whole thing and go and write another article for *The Irish Catholic*. That is not a joke. I do write for *The Irish Catholic*.

So bottom line…it has to be recorded that round this time I met another woman. Well, another particular woman. Let's call her Milly.

Milly became part of our marriage for a good few years. It was up and down. To say that things got fraught for awhile there in the middle is somewhat understating. But in retrospect it was worth it for all of us. In retrospect. I have found that screaming women smashing up furniture are much more fun in retrospect. But anyway. I'm pretty good at repairing furniture. And the stuff was rubbish anyway, it being a slum. And my number one wife and Milly got on well enough. But do get on better now. Well, I think so. Though maybe that's all male delusion. Certainly in later years when they met in supermarkets they chortled and giggled over their trollies. I kept my distance on those occasions. Perhaps because I didn't want to face the reality. It was me they were laughing at, and not the price of groceries.

And well they might. Because yes although I can josh at them and their onetime sapphic meanderings, it seems my activities are far more worthy of derision. My business enterprises. Yes, it was around this time that I went into the building industry. I felt I had experience. Had spent time years before in central Africa, going round on a motorbike, lightly armed with an automatic pistol and an even lighter UCD education, putting in drains and sanitation. All derelict now, that work. In retrospect I should have spent more time putting it to the local girls, to improve the ethnic stock. So to speak. Yes that is an outrageous racist remark. But what can I do? I put in drains and housing. Nearly got killed for my trouble. Drains and houses gone. Everyone dead. End of story. Certain experience and world view behind these typing fingers.

Going into the building industry has a good ring to it. The reality was I met a New Zealander with a ladder. I had a VW van, half converted to a camper. Planning to go to Italy. Didn't get there for another twenty five years. Not until the penultimate pages of this book in fact. New Zealander was broke, with a ladder. I was broke, with a van. The solution was obvious. We went into painting and decorating. And gradually extended. Garage conversions. Extensions. And on top of which I did a deal with the lawyer landlord to carry out repairs to his slum, and to his slum next door, and to offset this work against the rent. Doing very well until a woman got in the way. The woman was a gorgeous seventeen year old art student who needed a few bob. The living definition of a poppett, we hired her as a housepainter. Little white overalls, the whole bit. Lolita's older sister. Her tumbling hair tied up with string and splatters of emulsion on her cheeks. The New Zealander and I would watch her at work, thoughtfully.

Obsessively in love with H and Milly, I was content to admire the poppett from afar. My New Zealand partner was not. He ditched his own wife and son and set up home with the poppett in a flat on the Rock Road. And began to turn up for work in an irregular fashion. Then one day he didn't turn up to work at all. I called round. There he was in bed with the poppett, commuter traffic crawling past the door. I fulminated. We're meant to be in Stillorgan putting in a kitchen. What's the story?

He pointed to the sleeping poppett. She was the story. The partnership was dissolved on the spot. In some considerable acrimony. But he got his comeuppance. The Rock Road arrangement didn't last too long after. Poppetts are fickle. She dumped him and went to America. He went back to New Zealand with an english woman. His deserted wife stayed in Ireland and became a lecturer in women's studies in TCD. No really, I don't make this up, I wish I could, I'd make more money. So that was the end of the building business. And there's a woman in Stillorgan still waiting for a kitchen.

Sorry about that ma'am.

And about these photographs?

Well, the one is H, and the other is Milly. In a manner of speaking. Not really Milly of course, but the image is sort of standing in for her here. In looks they are very alike, apart from the hairstyle, dress sense and facial features. It's actually Princess Adelaide of Saxe Meiningen, she who gave her name to Adelaide Street. And what's all this about? Well, an earlier draft of this little book did feature a photo of Milly right here on this page and right here in this position, and in April of 2010 Milly and I met in a pub to discuss its inclusion. In the twenty or so years since the end of our affair she had gone her own way, became a successful woman and lived an interesting life, all that. It seems my leaving a woman can have a very beneficial effect.

The discussions about her role in this book went very very badly indeed. I left that pub a wiser man. Never offer a woman a two paragraph walk on part in a book of one hundred and thirty pages.

Women of Adelaide Street:
Princess Adelaide of
Saxe Meiningen and H.

Adelaide Street to Seafield Avenue

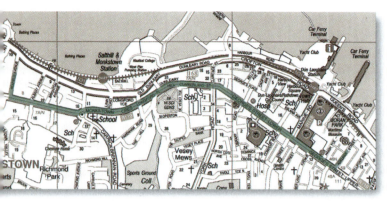

IT WAS DECIDED to move to Monkstown, to make a fresh start. It was to be one of many fresh starts. Why Monkstown, I have no idea. I suppose H's roots were there, such as they were. A soldier's daughter does not really have any roots. Born in Portlaoise, she had been brought up in the then military camp of Dublin's Beggars Bush Barracks. Before the army threw her widowed mother out. Her ethnic roots were Limerick, Tipperary. With a granny from Fermanagh. Essentially a culchie I suppose. A Monkstown culchie.

So off we went up Adelaide Street and out onto the main drag. And now years later I do it again, for the memories. A glance to the left reveals the Kingstown Mens Christian Institute. Essentially a temperance hall, this was founded in 1891 to cut down on Irish people drinking. How effective this was can best be judged in Temple Bar at two in the morning. Funnily enough I distinctly remember driving past the same institute one morning and seeing a pile of beer kegs waiting by the steps. That got me thinking. But to no great effect.

Right opposite the top of Adelaide Street is the Adelphi Centre. Once the site of the Adelphi Cinema, it is now a collection of office blocks of indeterminate function and design. The Swedish Ericcson Company still lurk in there, quietly making people redundant. Much like Leonie in Sweden made me redundant in Happaranda, quietly. Though I got no redundancy. But otherwise the blocks all seem empty and purposeless. Even before the property crash this was the case. It all has the air of an expensive mistake by some developers. Should I worry?

Funny thing, I cannot remember at all ever going to that vanished Adelphi Cinema with a woman. Seemed to be always in the Pavilion with them. Quirk of circumstance. What I

SRÁID SeOIRSe UAĊ.
GEORGE'S STREET, UPPER

can remember is going to the Adelphi with my former best friend. Lots of times. The heavily closeted homosexual who fancied me rotten. Himself and myself would go there frequently. He dragging his closet along and me giving him a hand with it like two furniture removers with a delicate item. I think it was at *The Magnificent Seven* that an important event occurred.

Yes, I know.

My audience here awaits agog.

I'm a tease.

Maybe that's why my former best friend fancied me.

The lights went up. The seats clattered back. People jostled into the aisles. And up along there from the direction of the screen limped a fuzzy haired bloke of a certain mien. I didn't know him from a hole in the wall but my former best friend and he were friends. Or at least acquaintances. Or had the same dealer, whatever. And that's how I met my friend Michael Powell. And he maintains that position, if not his fuzzy hair, to this very day. He goes as far back as to actually have come to my wedding. Not that I asked him. At that stage he was just another bloke I'd met around the place. He hadn't quite graduated to wedding guest material. But he had already been a friend of H so she asked him. Or maybe he was just a boyfriend of a friend of hers. Whatever, he made the cut.

A friend of hers as well as mine, they are both very literary, and read good books and discuss them. I rarely read books at all these days so leave them to it. It's bad enough having to read what I myself write. Certainly never read fiction anyway. A reviewer of my first novel said it looked like it was written by someone who's never read a novel. It was. Another bad review emerged from Nuala O Faoilean. Bad, self serving and inaccurate, like the story of her own life. Yet another female reviewer by the name of Julie Parsons was very scathing too. And took the whole thing personally. I'd never ever even met her. But she bumped into H at something or other, drew her aside, conspiritorally, said be careful, that man will kill you. I didn't. But Julie herself went on to write books about gruesome events. There may be issues there. I am available for consultation, usual fees. But anyway. I suppose the woman is to be commended for expanding the art of literary critique into the area of marriage guidance.

Moving along now towards the centre of the town. We have to admit that this part of the street is not at all bad, even now. Nice houses on the right, gardens and railings and brass plates on doors signalling the presence of solicitors and other incredibly boring business concerns. Nice, traditional. Why they haven't demolished the lot to build a *Lidl* or an *Aldi* is beyond me.

Haigh Terrace has a feel to it, and drags a passer by or at least the eye to the sea. But not today. Just time for me to remember that my great grandmother Jane Carroll lived down there. Fallen on hard times in one of those flats where Edwardian women waited to die. A single sepia photo in a silver frame on the windowsill. Fading and faded like her memories.

The former Royal Bank now, built in 1871, designed by Charles Geoghegan. A fabric shop. I like a fabric shop in a town. But then, my mother's family were tailors going back many generations. It's in the blood. And there's good shops along the left hand side. And then McDonalds. More or less my favourite restaurant, I am not a gourmet. My friend Michael is. As is H. He takes her out to gourmet meals in fancy restaurants. They discuss literature. I stay at home, creating it. Works all round.

McDonald's used be Lees furniture when I was a little boy. A jungle of sofas and furniture, all far taller than me. I'd hide from my mother, but she always found me. The realisation that I'd have to go to a real jungle to escape her is probably what drove me to Africa. Dunnes Stores next, and that was the main part of Lees Department Store. Upstairs was *The Avenue Hotel*. Behind there in Dungar Terrace lived my great uncle Bob and his sister Kathy. He wore a bowler hat and I don't think she was quite the full shilling. They left my mother their house. And when my mother got dementia we spent the money on her nursing home. It sort of all fits together in a way.

In 2009 I read planning notices on the windows all along here. Dunnes are going to knock everything down except the front facade. And build a megastore behind. Let's hope it keeps fine for them. Pity builders didn't do the same on the other side, maintain the facades.

That monstrous shopping centre is really very ugly. I don't know what the architecture critic Pevsner would have said, but *give us a break here* is my comment. It's terrible, the demolished buildings were so nice, all late victorian and red brick, a lively mishmash of Queen Anne, Dutch Classical, the lot. Not to mention the famous old Roman Café more or less around the present entrance to the centre. Famous? Well, for ice cream anyway. Whatever.

Bóthar na Mara
MARINE ROAD

There was an architectural bounce and oneness about the whole place. And the old St Michael's Church was a drama, scripted in soaring stone and glowing glass. And there were dark corners inside to mirror the dark corners of the soul. A church needs that. But the place burned down. I was in Africa at the time. A friend sent me a postcard. St Michael's has burned down. He was so pleased. But then he wasn't an architect, he was a barrister. Struck off since. Had it coming.

That postcard came at a serendipity time. Most messages do in fact, because there is a oneness in the happenings of a person's life. I was up on the Copperbelt then, and had done drawings for the Jehovah's Witnesses, for the Kingdom Hall they wanted to build in the town. Just the technical stuff, they didn't need any more help. No way did they need any help. When the time came they gathered from miles around, arriving on motorbikes and pickup trucks and bicycles, and some on foot. And put up their Kingdom Hall over a weekend. I watched them, the enthusiasm, the togetherness and laughter. And that postcard from Dún Laoghaire in my mind. What the fuck, I thought. How could somebody be pleased that God's house was destroyed, and the prayers of dead generations lost to the sky?

Yes I was in Africa when the old church burned down. But I was right there inside the new one when the foundation stone was blessed by Archbishop Dermot Ryan. In later times I was to meet the very bishop. Tall and ascetic, and of frosty mien, I shook his hand. It was limp and dangling. I felt like I was lying on the ground and hanging on to the tail of a bullock. But it was far from shaking bishops' hands that I was at the opening of the church. My former best friend and I had been on our way to Walters Pub. We had seen a mob go in the door and followed them. There goes the mob, I suppose. I am its writer, I must follow them.

Whatever. There's a plaque inside the door about all this. No, just recording the ceremony, not mentioning specifically that I was there. Or that my former best friend was standing right beside me in his closet. And both of us anxious to continue our journey to Walters. Nowadays when I visit Dún Laoghaire I always go into the new church, to light candles for my Granny who was married in the old one. And look for dark corners to mirror the dark corners of my soul. But there are none. So I just kneel and pray to gods who guide me on my way. Not very successfully, it must be said. Prayer and asking for directions when lost in Leitrim can have a lot in common. But I go through the motions. And the Catholic in me blesses himself. But I always notice that the inner Protestant never genuflects. He just walks silently past the altar.

Leaving the church I pause beside that memorial plaque. I read the words and think of other words and other times. And words and memories play their melody. But sometimes in St Michael's I realise that it's not their melody at all. It's just Rumanian knackers playing accordeons up the street outside Penneys. Penneys that was once Findlaters, where my Granny shopped. No Rumanians then, no Granny now.

This street is what happens when a town dies. We're seriously into charity shop territory here now. A strange and alien world. But inspiring in a way. Certainly inspiring me to rush back home and dump the entire contents of my house into a skip, lest anything ends up in the maws of Oxfam. I'll not have those shifty suburbanites rummaging through my stuff. They're looking for *Antique Road Show* bargains, that lot. Can smell the greed off of them. They won't find any bargains though. My children will have picked the place clean. *Dad promised to give me that*, I hear them say. *He knew I always liked it.* No he didn't promise any such bloody thing. And all he knew was that it was worth a few bob.

Ah sure kids, dont'cha love 'em. No choice here. Along this charity shop promenade you're seriously ordered to love them, the little black and brown ones, and the ones with asian eyes. I'm not crazy about that sort of advertising. No more than I'm crazy about people having Philipina maids, African gardeners. I don't go for the caste system, even if we do call it multiculturalism. May not be intended, but it's just another word for racism. All words that end in *ism* tend to mean the same.

Walk on, remembering. When I lived in Africa I never noticed the colour of children. Though I suppose they noticed mine. Walk on, into Johnny Goodbody's bookshop. Discuss the difficulties of making any sort of living from books. Selling them, writing them. It's a mug's game. But booksellers and book writers alike have to play some game I suppose. It keeps them off the streets. I reckon that round here a lot more people could be kept off the streets. There's challenging demographics. Petty criminals, addicts, dealers, their own beaux walk. There's them, but I suppose just mostly only ordinary poor people. Under pressure. Strange that Dún Laoghaire has so many poor. The richest part of Ireland. Something not…quite…adding up… methinks.

Walk on. The shops flip by like cards in a conjuror's hands. There goes the Queen of Hearts. And there is Hick's. Bought sausages there. And they did a particular kind of pork chop, great for sweet and sour. The cards flicker on. And here's the Ace of Diamonds. O'Connors. Jewellery. Never bought H any jewellery there. Couldn't afford it. But from cheap joints and from stalls I bought her rings and things. At one stage she was so heavily decorated it was like going to bed with a christmas tree. But she's never had a real engagement ring. The sort for friends to *oohhh* and *aahh* about. We were too poor for any of that. And later there didn't seem much point. Though when my mother died I did try to buy her ring from the estate. But some of my sisters vetoed the notion. I had a lot of money by then, and offered thousands of euro. And normally with my sisters money talks, big time. But my offer was declined. Why? I can only surmise. Some sentimental reasoning unexplainable? Or maybe some kind of class thing, H never having been quite Killiney enough for the posher element in my sisterhood ? Whatever. They have their reward.

Moving on. And to the right are to be seen two premises that featured strongly in my earlier banking arrangements. This was the hub of finance for many of us Dún Laoghaire citizens in past days, our Wall Street, our City of London. Yes, those buildings there were the onetime dole office, and that conveniently situated beside the onetime McManus Pawnshop. And opposite them on the left the famous Thompson Furniture, all Swedish and swish and brave new world of design. My mate George Bennett from Dalkey married a Thompson girl. But died quite young. And in 2009 I wrote about him in my column in *The Irish Times*. And two of his children emailed me in thanks. Strange and nice how gracious some people are…even in these difficult days.

Bloomfields now on our left. Never quite got Bloomfields, never knew exactly where it was at. It just did not impinge. Except that they knocked down a convent to build it. Is that crazy or what? Why would you knock down a convent to build an empty shopping centre where no-one wants to go? Why not leave the empty convent buildings, spooky with dead nuns? Creaky wooden corridors and the smell of old polish and the smell of dead flowers. And statues of women saints with chains of rosaries round their hands and wrists. That's bondage they're playing there, with their creator master. It's all so creepy and meaningful. And should have been preserved. Those images of women with snakes curling round bare ankles and up their legs, like something from a psychiatrist's textbook. A town needs that atmosphere. It's real. Sooner or later young girls would come again to enter and to pray. To play bondage with their creator, it's in their nature. They sure as hell won't go to an empty shopping centre. Except to buy tights maybe.

Bloomfields, Dunphy's Pub, St Michael's Hospital. The three of them. Some kind of Holy Trinity thing going on in the head round here. God the Bloomfields. God the Dunphy's Pub. And God the St Michael's Hospital.

Indeed. God. St Michael's Hospital. It dates back to 1874. Designed by John Loftus Robinson and built for the Sisters of Mercy, it was apparantly noted for its advanced design. Yeah right. It was noted for other things in my lifetime. The place enjoyed a fearsome reputation. It had gruesome standards of nursing, cleanliness and medical procedure. Made *Our Lady of Lourdes* in Drogheda look like *The Mayo Clinic*. A particular resident surgeon was mentioned in hushed terms. Much in the manner of Transylvanian peasants whispering the name of Dracula in ghoulish movies. Practically everyone in Dún Laoghaire seemed to know or be related to someone this guy had killed or maimed. Mention of the fact that a friend or relative was going in to St Michael's was met with thoughtful worried frown. As of someone who didn't really want to say anything. But thought you should be warned nonetheless. St Michael's truly defined that difficult philosophic term, existential dread.

My friend Michael is prone to existential dread, big time. He and I and H and his then wife Mary…I've never had a *then wife*, wonder how it feels…we were sitting in Dunphy's Pub opposite the hospital one merry evening. Planning to hit some expensive restaurant with our gourmet palates. Well, their gourmet palates. As mentioned, I'm McDonalds to the core. Suddenly my friend Michael crashed to the ground, curled up in agony. Myself and H and his then wife carted him across the road to St Michael's. Don't take me in there, he kept gasping. In existential dread. But, not knowing what else to do, we had to ignore the pleadings.

It turned out he had a collapsed lung. Being prone to that sort of thing, having had polio as a child. The hospital told him and us that they'd be carrying out procedures. Not on me you won't, said Michael, lepping out of his trolley and crawling off across the floor. Procedures was a very bad word when associated with the concept of St Michaels. You had a fifty fifty chance of surviving procedures. The upshot of all this was that Michael, gasping into a phone, ordered a private ambulance to rescue him and take him to Vincents for procedures. I don't think St Michael's were any too pleased. It's a pride thing. They'd sooner a corpse leave by the back door than a patient escape out the front.

I myself spent a few days in St Michael's, in the intensive care unit. This was a learning curve. Everyone around me died. I suppose people in ICU's do die. But this struck me as being a bit out of proportion. Then it all made sense after one particular night. The bloke beside

NOTICE
NO LIABILITY SHALL ATTACH TO THE BOARD OF THIS HOSPITAL FOR ANY DAMAGE OR LOSS, HOWEVER CAUSED TO PERSONS

me in the next bed got a cardiac arrest. Crash teams and crash trollies crashed through the door. The trolley with the heart starting machine… I'm not a cardiologist, whatever they call the yoke…that was plugged in. Stand back, said the doctor. Everyone stood back. Nothing happened, no electricity. A nurse kicked the plug. Still nothing happened. Oh yes she said, they were looking at that this afternoon. I thought they'd fixed it. They hadn't. The trolley was dead. As shortly would soon be the patient. Nice bloke too. Mother of Jesus. But that was of course ten years ago. I hear things have improved since. I have no first hand knowledge of this alleged improvement, and intend to make no effort to gain such.

On top of everyone around me dying, and the definite possibility of my doing likewise, my stay in St Michael's was not at all a good time. I was not quite prepared to meet my maker. But hopefully have made significant improvements on that score since. This psychological situation was compounded by the fear that a particular St Michael's nurse would come through the door. A particular nurse whom I'd last seen in a Clarinda Park bedsitter a quarter of a century previous. With whom I'd multi tasked. Tasks included drinking wine from O'Brien's off licence, eating a chinese takeaway from Mr Yungs, unpeeling clothes from her slender form like a thoughtful monkey with some exotic fruit. And listening to Leonard Cohen singing Suzanne lives alone in a shack by the river.

In the hospital, in deranged and dying state, I decided that this nurse had now risen to great heights in the hierarchy. That she was no longer slim. And that I hadn't kept some bargain made back there in Clarinda Park. I probably hadn't. Bargains are the empty wine bottles of such nights. To be recycled in the morning with someone else. Yes. I decided. It was obvious. I knew yes just knew that she was going to come right through that door. With a grudge, a score to even. That she was going to look like a cross between Hattie Jacques in *Carry On Nurse* and one of those Austrian nurses that get arrested for killing eighty five patients. They always seem to be Austrians. Austrians worry me. If they're not keeping girls in cellars to shag they're involved in mass murder. But that, like the East Link Bridge, is beside the point. (I have to make jokes like that, Hugh Leonard is dead). I knew in that bed that I was going down. Big time. But of course she wasn't around. She didn't arrive. And no doubt she had long since left the hospital. And was in Saudi Arabia making gin in a bathtub, organising expatriate wife swapping parties. Or something. Whatever nurses of a certain age do.

Men of a certain age walk on.

Dún Laoghaire sort of peters out after the hospital. There is little of note. And less of memory. There are few historical facts to record. Except maybe that the old town hall was in the building opposite the end of Library Road, now a furniture shop. It was formerly Perry's, a ship's chandlers. In my sailing days I used go there for boating stuff. Shackles and things. To shackle things. That is a lovely word. It almost rhymes with chuckle. But not, I suppose, if you're a slave.

There's the library itself down here, Carnegie. And the onetime Workmen's Club, now an office building. What's with all these offices, one wonders? What's wrong with the internet, broadband? Why are we building for yesterday? Why am I asking daft questions. Walk on. When a street peters out I'm none too sure of the word to describe its continuation. But continue it does. But if a street can be likened to a person then this street here is like a person with Alzheimers. It's still Georges Street Lower, but it doesn't really know its name. Or its purpose. Or the fact that there exists names and purposes in the scheme of things. It is dreadfully sad.

And I'm none too sure if it cheers up once turned into Cumberland Street.

But a word about this crossroads first. The shop on the left at the corner of York Road was in long gone days Bill Kearney's record shop. And here I bought Paul Anka singing *Oh Pleeese Di aaaana*...not to mention Elvis and his *Jailhouse Rock*. interesting record shop, of a type of the times, with little telephone like things along the counter to check out the music before purchase. Dim memories of rows of teenagers sitting there holding these yokes to their ears in thoughtful silence. They are middleaged people now, sitting on the Dart, going to work with Ipods in their ears.

Onwards, the view of Cumberland Street ahead is none too inspiring. But historical perspective is required. Those small and cramped looking little houses actually replaced dreadful courts of cabins and teetering warehouses crammed with humanity. Except when everyone got cholera. That emptied them out a bit. The cabins were thatched and barefoot children splashed around in puddles full of floating turds. It wasn't good. It was *Slumdog Millionaire* meets *Riverdance*. And these abysmal conditions were not just here along Cumberland Street. The slums ringed all around the fine town of Kingstown, like a bell around a clapper. Ask not, as my old mate John Donne once said, ask not for whom that bell tolled. But continue, and Cumberland Street sort of explodes into a sort of openness and views of harbour and skies and the city beyond.

Down along here we are now walking along the cliff top over the old Dunleary harbour. That signposted hill is actually the route of the stream that flowed into the harbour, and still does beneath the tarmac. I mentioned

that. But that was several years ago, we were only on our way to Adelaide Street. Three in a bed sex romps and all that. And I accept that the reader may have forgotten the stream. Foolish perhaps. An ancient sparkling stream buried in a drain is actually far more interesting to dwell upon than other's sexual peculiarities.

Correction, we are not precisely on the cliff top here. We are threading our way along half way up, because the hill rises still up to our left. DeVesci Terrace up there, with huge statues of Castor and Pollux looking out over private tennis courts. These guys were the brothers of Helen of Troy. Twins, but by different fathers. Pollux was immortal, and Castor was mortal. Castor died, but Pollux asked Zeus to let him share some of his immortality. Zeus obliged, and the twins are now the Gemini constellation. Well that's what the Greeks reckoned. But of course this concept goes back long before the Greeks. The notion of divine twins is a recurring theme in proto-indo-european mythology. It goes way back, and indeed it also comes forward to us. The Christian soul is our Castor, so to speak, and Pollux our earthly form. My book *Ancient Ireland* touches on these matters. I actually do know this stuff. But haven't a bull's notion as to why the two buckos are in statues up on top of DeVesci Terrace. All I know is that they are up there, looking out over the trees towards Dublin. Out over the trees of the little woods which hide somewhere the site of *Juggy's Well*. The forgotten *Juggy's Well*. And to think of it reminds me that I once wrote books about ancient Ireland, but my readership declined. So I moved on.

Monkstown Crescent now and the onetime home of my grandfather

Frederick Kennedy. Number four here was the house where little
Jeannette Kennedy died of scarlatina aged 11. Maybe her
bedroom lies behind that top window. And maybe there
they laid her little body out, all in white I suppose. I see
that as I pass. And undertakers carrying in the little white coffin. And
laying her in it and closing linen over her face like a wedding veil. And
then bringing it back down the stairs to their horse drawn hearse. The
sort of hearse much favoured by gangsters and members of the travelling
community these days. But back then commonplace. With black horses
and, for a child like Jeannette, white plumes on the horses' heads.

She had no mother then, her mother had died in Adelaide Street.
But I suppose there were women to weep beside my grandfather. Aunts

and sisters and cousins. He would not have wept, that
man. He was cold and hard, and none too honest in
his business dealings. Shortly he would marry another
woman, and then another, and become extremely
wealthy. And move from Monkstown Crescent to
Frescati House in Blackrock. A great mansion which
once stood on the site of the Frescati shopping centre.
And there he had grooms and cooks and maids and
nannies for his many children, one of whom was my
father. He had all that, old Frederick Kennedy. But he
didn't have Jeannette. She was a ghost. A ghost back
there in Adelaide Street. Waiting. Waiting for another
ghost, the ghost of my own daughter Siobhán to arrive from America.
Someone to play with. Out there on the street on sunny afternoons, and
in winter in those gaslit rooms.

Walk on.

H and I had a second child, Alex. We sent him to the boarded up
school around the corner here. Though of course it wasn't boarded up
then. Except in protestantism. Miss Hadnett the head told me she didn't
believe in multi denominational schools. Though of course she did let our
catholic kid in, but that was to keep the numbers up. 'Multidenominational'
she said, sternly, 'means no denomination at all'. And of course she was
right. A fine and good woman. And dead since. God be good to her, as
they say now where I live. One wonders what she would think of her
school now boarded up. We cannot know, but fortunately we can know
what I think. It's an eyesore and a bloody disgrace. And makes a mockery

of the prayers in the church alongside. Get a grip prods. If you cant think what to do with the building then give it to some African church. That'll praise the Lord.

Moving along, hoping my advice to the Representative Church Body is appreciated and speedily acted upon, we are heading now up the Monkstown Road. Its straightness and length would imply that it's one of those military built roads,

but I don't know that for sure. I don't know lots of things for sure. But I do know for sure that here on the left in Purbeck Lodge lived Dick Cameron, an American folk singer. From Concord Massachussetts, he was a big, good looking and charming sort of bloke. Played guitar, and sang like Burl Ives. But he was a bullshitter of cosmic proportions. He fancied H and told her that she was 'like a flower waiting to be opened'. He was of course trying to get into her knickers. But sentences with flowers and waiting and opening in them are the worst and least effective sort of thing for a man to say to the likes of H. If he wants to seduce her. After all, she was born in Portlaoise. Not that Dick Cameron could have been expected to know that.

"I couldn't be doing with that shit", she would say. In fact she did say it, reporting the flower awaiting to be opened bit back to her husband. As of course a dutiful wife should. Having been married to her for several years at the time, I didn't find this very complimentary to my own flower opening capabilities. But whatever. H kept her flower closed to Cameron, and put on double locks, just to be sure. He later found religion and died quite young.

If he'd come up with a better chat-up line he might have lived a little longer.

SEAFIELD AVENUE

EGLINTON LODGE, SEAFIELD AVENUE

FROM THE BUILDING BUSINESS it was one small step for man and a giant one etc for us. We bought a fleet of caravans. From some years back on our return from America we had had an empty mobile home sitting on a sand dune site in Arklow. This was costing us money so we decided to rent it out. And, no good in renting one mobile home out, let's get lots. We got three more. A modest fleet. Our customers mostly came from Northern Ireland for holiday lettings. It was ok. But one hell of a drag going back and forth to Arklow every weekend to repair the damages. Let in new tenants. That sort of thing. We also did girl guides' groups from East Wall. They say that paedophiles just cannot be cured. But I have a theory that putting them in close proximity to gangs of girl guides from East Wall might go a considerable way in that direction.

Back on the south side, residence wise, we moved a bit upmarket. Not much, it was a basement flat here. And the landlady was an extremely unpleasant woman. A bitter old bat, she liked the rent we paid but wasn't too keen on us. But in fairness to the dead, we did start a mushroom farm in one of the basement rooms. Whether this had anything to do with her dislike I just do not know. I suspect she just disliked (insert anything and/or everything). Pity. The mushrooms seemed such a good idea. The place was ideally dark and damp and off we went and bought grow-your-own-mushrooms sacks in a garden centre. We would sell the surplus. Big bucks. But the mushrooms failed to grow. Never understood why. Maybe they didn't want to be in the same building as that landlady.

Our allegiances had now been transferred from the Carney Arms to Goggins Pub. In addition to being a caravan mogul, I was working for Stephenson Gibney. A very large and very corrupt architectural firm in Dublin. Whole departments were involved in activities requiring brown envelopes. The client list was a who's who of future Ansbacher tribunals and the likes. Sam was charming and an egregious crook. His partner Arthur was neither so charming nor so obviously bent. Just hid both traits better. I preferred Sam. In later years they made Gibney President of the RIAI. For not being caught, I suppose.

I sat beside Marian Finucane. But every time I hear her on the radio

I see someone else. Another worker, Jim Malcolm, raising a sardonic eye to heaven at her conversation. He lived in Monkstown, and became one of my drinking companions there. And we bought a rowing boat together. But Goggins for Jim all went sour when one evening he insisted on stroking H's thigh. "Stop stroking her thigh", I requested politely. But I may very well have phrased it differently. He declined. He said H had two thighs and I could stroke the other. No way. Three in a bed is one thing but three on a lounge bar banquette is another. The owner of the thighs sat calmly watching as Jim's fingers inched upwards on her leg. I reckon she calculated a fight to break out before her virtue came under serious threat. A Sacred Heart Convent girl, they can judge these things to a tee. She calculated right. The fight broke out. Tumbling tables and chairs and glasses and all that. God those were the fun times. And we were all thrown out into the night. But we made up and went back to Jim's place, a third floor flat on Trafalgar Terrace. I can't remember what happened then, thigh wise. But I do recall Jim pissing out the window on to the street below.

Drink? Involved. He never did get to back to Goggins. But I lived on and mended my fences with the proprietor, Joe Keegan. As mad as a hatter, he was later to drop dead playing tennis. Personally I think he was far too old for tennis. Which really should only be played by young people aged from about sixteen to maybe twenty five. Young female people. With nice legs and short skirts. Seems the only point of the game really.

Not sure if Goggins Pub has a good vibe. There's lots of haunted people there, with empty bitter lives. Awaiting inevitable but inexplicable tragedies, lots of them. Yes I know that can apply to most Dublin suburban pubs, but Goggins more than slightly more than the others. I have a theory that it's built on the graves of those monks from Carrickbrennan Road. Some kind of bad psychic glitch going on there anyway. Jim Malcolm himself was killed in a traffic accident. Good bloke. Pity. And a good taste in thighs too, I realise as I click this image into place on the screen. And I wonder if his buried finger bones remember wandering there. Do bones remember flesh?

H in Seafield Avenue

GOGGINS PUB, MONKSTOWN

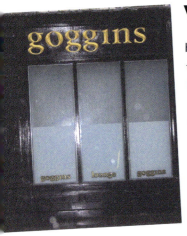

WE NEVER ACTUALLY LIVED IN GOGGINS, it just seemed that way. It wasn't that we drank that much, we couldn't. H had a baby and a job. I had a job and the caravan business. And, come to think, and to be totally new man about the matter, I suppose I had a baby too. Goggins was more of a social centre.

A good pub in those days, I suppose. A onetime grocery shop, with bar tucked in the back as there used be in country towns. But that long before my time in Monkstown. Though not in that of H who'd been a child round here. 'My mother used buy groceries here', she would say, thoughtfully watching ice cubes melt into her vodka.

'Ah hah', I would reply.

Yes, it's definitely true what they say.

Conversation does bring a couple closer together.

Goggins was generally middleclass, but with a working class enclave. And each class divided up into age groups and interests. Not to mention divided up into one's relative proximity to rampant alcoholism.

All in all, a strictly hierarchical place.

We were in one little group, and there was another, an older crowd than us. People in forties, fifties. They clustered at a particular place along the bar near the door. A coterie, as of a golf club bar. Dentists, lawyery sort of people. They talked of rugby, quite a lot. And maybe they actually did play golf betimes. But it was clear that the centres of their lives was those four yards of Goggins counter.

I spent a lot of time watching them.

Listened, overheard.

I noted that even though they were dentist and lawery sort of people, they allowed into their circle more or less anyone so long as they were drunks. I saw this, and I took mental note of their strange rituals. How they made ascerbic comments about one another. But in high good humour pulled over barstools for the newcomer. And in bad humour tightened the circle when one of their number went home. Strange that vague resentment in the tightening of the circle, as if they had been betrayed. And I saw how each played parts. One was the grumpy old bugger. And another the middle aged vamp, still hanging in there, showing legs on her barstool. And another was this and another was that, and I didn't want to be any of them.

I noted all that.

One day (I thought) H and I will be like them. Unless we change.

We changed.

Neither of us became alcoholics. Even though both of us, being native Irish, came fully equipped with alcoholic dna in the genetic heritage. But nonetheless we did *enjoy drink in a sensible manner*, as the ads prissily urge folks these days. Even *enjoying drink in a sensible manner* there were all sorts of interesting social interactions. And we could always get drinking companions. Though perhaps that only because H has large breasts and a friendly interested manner. Whatever. I suppose it was all very lively and interesting in a pub and going places after sort of way. (Yes, these paragraphs here have been heavily censored. By the very same H who took a friendly and interested interest in the earlier drafts.)

In retrospect anyway, I'm not at all sure how much time or money was available for social butterflying in those days. We were very very busy. There were many money making schemes afoot, and we were both very occupied. H had taken up a career as a store detective. And spent long hours lurking around Arnotts and Boyers and suchlike. But of course in no time at all the entire shoplifting demographic of Dublin knew who she was. But it was reckoned that her role was to deter, rather than to catch in act. Coming in at five foot one and being of gentle and girlie disposition, I suppose this was just as well. As for myself, I still had the van from the building days and, with the replacement of a few seats, it had now morphed into the transport for a band known as *Supply Demand* and *Curve*. I was the driver, roadie, and humper of musical equipment in and out of provincial venues. I also had to sit around during the gigs, staying sober to drive the band back to Dublin in the small hours. Luckily the band were reasonably musical, and had a pretty good musician, Jolyon Jackson, involved. Still and all, those many nights of observing *Supply Demand* and *Curve*, not to mention their audience, that put the soul in a thoughtful and introspective place. From which I'm not at all sure it has yet emerged.

Funny old place, the artistic thing. As a writer I suppose I'm looking at my own calling as an insider, and don't see how depressing and miserable our lives can be. However, looking at musicians, it all becomes clear. Of creative and artistic bent the same as us scribblers, they're in a woegeous situation. And we their quieter mirrors. I plan one day to write a few hundred thousand words on the commodification of art…but am waiting until the dementia kicks in a bit more strongly. Enough to note that as I write these words here…I'm in San Remo, the sun is shining…as I write of long gone Goggins days there's a parallel window on my laptop with an email telling me that Dave McHale has died in Frankfurt.

Musician Dave McHale of Goggins. Well, Dave McHale of *Boomtown Rats* and *Stepaside* and all that. Apparantly he has died at fifty eight and Bob Geldof will be playing a special memorial gig for him at the rugby club in Stradbrook Road. Bob wrote a *Boomtown Rats'* song, (Dave), for him, when his girlfriend killed herself with heroin.

Time heals, Believe, Then it will seem you dreamed these things, Long Ago.

Yeah. Right Bob.

And sorry Dave, I can't be there.

And anyway you wouldn't listen to me.

I often told you a man over forty should never wear jeans.

It's not dignified.

Though what in hell is dignity?

Move on.

Remember.

We changed, and drifted away from Goggins. Not least because of the presence of musicians, and because it was boring. And because of the threat of alcoholism, it was dangerous. So we went to different places, adopted different interests. Mine was mainly her. Don't wear this, wear that, too low a top, not low enough, that sort of thing. She'd model for me, twirl around. And say make up your fucking mind. Later on she bought a wig, of different style and colour hair, to change her look completely. It changed her look completely. I watched her then, amazed. I realised I hadn't married only H. She could be every bloody letter in the alphabet.

We went different places.

So that's the way it was. And yes, the expression *that couple were in need of serious therapy* does occur. But we weren't. And we're not. We are actually very quiet and home loving sort of people. Always true to each other darling in our fashion. And perhaps with some slightly eccentric habits, but terribly ordinary and conservative. We read *The Daily Telegraph*. And H votes *Fine Gael*.

GONE WEST

ESCAPE FROM THE SOUTH SIDE. We got rid of the caravans business and bought a ruin of a house in the West of Ireland. And migrated there with our second baby, Alex. It was all pretty far from suburban Dublin. Water from a pump. With additional supplies coming through the holes in the roof. But that remains another story. Things got a bit complicated. Her name was Ann. But she went her way. And I couldn't cope anyway. H was my sun and I was a little parched planet circling her. And Milly was still ongoing. Though now more as duty than as pleasure. There's only so much. So Ann went. Then after after a year or so in the west H and I came back to the south side. Very wet, and very broke. But managed to rent a semi off Rochestown Avenue in Glenageary. Well, folks there call it Glenageary. I had always thought it was in Sallynoggin myself. But then, I was born in Killiney. And up there we are very, very, snobbish.

116 JOHNSTOWN AVENUE, GLENAGEARY

HERE WE EXPERIMENTED with being a regular suburban couple. It didn't work out that well, not really. But I did manage to set up a bit of an architectural business, and H started working in the publishing industry. We did our best. It has to be said we dressed the part. Never mind that this photo facing here reminds me of those British couples one sees in the Lake District or up Mount Snowdon in matching anoraks. My excuse…it was taken on a boat. The Waverley Paddle Steamer. Hence the coats and scarves and general aren't-we-having-lots-of-fun demeanour.

And about that hat?

There is a story to that hat. Not long after this photo was taken I was in Ballina railway station and approached by a man. In younger days I was often approached by men in railway stations.

But that was usually in continental Europe on my wanderings. Maybe I should stop this sentence right here. So. Anyway. Ballina. In hat. Approached by man. He looked at me. "Hello George", he said, grinned, mightily pleased with himself, and departed.

The train journey from Ballina to Dublin is a lonesome and a thoughtful pilgrimage. Half of it can be summed up in one word, Ballyhaunis. And the other half in another, Portarlington. And both of these words can be joined up in a verbless two word sentence to explain the melancholy, the despair, the futility and incompetence, and the sheer wish-I-was-dead alcoholism of our island race.

It's also a very long journey. And very expensive. And I'm sick of it. And if I live long enough to get the free travel I'll probably only do it just the once again, just to see how it feels, travelling free from Dublin to Ballina. I suspect it's going to feel much the same. Monotonous. But of course punctuated by incident and persons met of telling and instructive import. But I can't fit them all in. My book designer tells me I have only eight hundred words available on these two pages here. One wonders if Tolstoy or even Joyce would have bowed to the strictures of a book designer, but times have changed I suppose. And none of us are free. So I can really only deal with one incident of telling and instructive import.

It concerns a schoolteacher from Belmullet. A woman in her thirties. The train was quiet. She sat opposite with her feet up on the seat beside me. We were travelling in the Dublin to Mayo direction. Hardly matters which, but one must set a scene. We got on very well. By Castlerea I was playing with her toes. And considering her ankles. Courtesy of Iarnród Éireann I was in a foot fetishist's heaven, enhanced by changing scenery. If the line had been extended to Belmullet... as indeed was the original scheme for the track... then god knows what would have happened. But the point of this telling and instructive tale is that it has a sombre ending. Because not so long ago I met a young woman. In her twenties. She was from Belmullet. We talked. Her mother was a teacher. In Belmullet. I found out names. I put two and two together. Did you know, I told her, did you know that twenty years ago I played with your mother's toes on the train from Dublin to Ballina? She laughed merrily. And I smiled. But a wan smile and a rather sad smile about the melancholy of time. And its passing. All that.

But the hat, the hat?

I got back to Johnstown Avenue and said to H.

A man came up to me in Ballina Station.

Uh huh, she said.

And he said Hello George, and walked away. What's that all about?

She laughed. And pointed out that George was a character in the then RTÉ soap *Glenroe*. And George wore a hat just like mine. I remembered. A very irritating character played by the very irritating actor Alan Stanford. It always amazes that, whilst Ireland exports A list people to Britain to do very well, they only export their B listers here. Why is that? The Alan Stanfords and Bruce Arnolds and Gillian Bowlers. They're B listers, if not C.

No-one would pay the slightest attention to them in their own country. The phenomenon seems to be a British-Irish thing. We get A listers from other countries, Poles, Americans, Congolese, from everywhere. But only the mediocre from Britain. Why is this? Legacy of colonialism, we'll put it down to that. Or the sheer ignorance, stupidity and fawning servility of our colonised island race. Whatever.

The hat?

I never wore it again.

Johnstown Avenue to Flower Grove

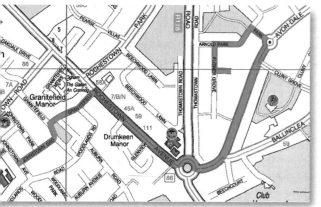

THE JOURNEY from Johnstown Avenue to Flower Grove did for me. I hit the wall. Writer's block. I couldn't think of anything to say. It was the winter of 2008. I sat there in the Italian evening, H popping olives into my mouth with jewel draped fingers tipped in scarlet red. And topping up my wineglass to my nod. All that.

It is that time of evening.

We are in Ceriana in Italy. We are staying in an apartment high up in the old town. People who have been in Ceriana will know what I mean. It's a long walk up. A bloody long way. We've brought groceries and wine and stuff. Neither of us are young. We are tired. A few years down the road and we will be older, more tired. And a few years more and one of us will be dead. And the fact of that is neither good nor bad, that is the way of it.

It is that time of evening.

I sip my wine and try to think of what to write about the journey from Johnstown Avenue to Flower Grove. But there's a longer different journey drifting in my mind. And back at the start of that I am sitting in a coffeebar in Dún Laoghaire. And a schoolgirl comes through the door. And I say to myself I will marry her, I knew that. Not because she's a schoolgirl. But because long times in the future I will be with her, in Ceriana in Italy. She will be tired, middle aged. She will be different. She will have the figure of a woman who has had five children. Five of my children.

It is that time of evening.

She has kicked off her shoes. I remember how I kissed and chewed at those tired toes. When they were younger. Her feet know this as they look at me. And I wander around the apartment, trying to think of what to write about the journey between Johnstown Avenue and Flower Grove. And I touch her knees as I pass her by. And she smiles. And later on it's very hot in bed. And she wears a sheet and throws it off. And I flap at the sheet to make a breeze, to make her cool. And we wake in the morning to the sound of Italian poultry, and the sound of a Vespa puttering up the hill. And she lies there in the bend of my arm, trusting me. And she is my child and my lover and my mother. And I grin to myself. But the grin sort of fades when I remember what I'm trying to do, my work for the day ahead. Because a few months back I had started writing a short snappy book. Just for the hell of it. A book which I called *a walk on the south side*. And decided that it'd be a love story. And that was the easy bit. But not so easy to think of anything to say about the journey from Johnstown Avenue to Flower Grove.

No, there was nothing for it.

Serious field research was required.

Back in Ireland the serious field research was undertaken. This involved me getting into a car and driving to Johnstown Avenue. And from there to Flower Grove. And back again.

Numerous times. Granted, this was slightly more interesting than it would have been at the time when we did move house. Back that time I didn't get lost. The road between the Graduate and Deerhunter Pubs wasn't built then, and you could nip around by the shopping centre into Thomastown Road and thence Flower Grove. Nowadays the route seems to be half way down Avondale Road and back up. It took me awhile to work this out. I don't have a satnav. Though I'd actually rather like a satnav. Very fond of gizmos. And I find those calm satnav voices rather soothing to the mind. Bring to memory the voices of nurses in intensive care units. Two o'clock in the morning sort of times. They soothe. Even though you know the truth. They're hoping that the laying you out is not going to make them late home for breakfast.

Getting lost around Arnold Park and Bellevue Road may seem to be fairly ridiculous. But then, getting lost is some kind of existential condition, rather than bearing any relationship to geography. I think perhaps that getting lost is another phrase for not wanting to be found. And in all honesty I don't want to be found anywhere between Johnstown Road and Flower Grove. I never really did. Yes I know that knocking suburbs and suburban people is worth a few hundred words to any Irish writer, but I never subscribed to that. Several reasons. One is practical, people in suburbs are the ones who buy books.

It's incredible, the number of people who don't buy books. The farming folks who live round me in Mayo are not at all big into books. "What're you doing", says me a couple of years back, watching a farmer neighbour piling a pile of books in his yard. "Clearing the attic", says he, getting ready to light a bonfire. An illegal bonfire, but we wouldn't be worrying much about that stuff around here. And if it annoys the Green Party it's good enough for us.

There's something horribly fascinating about watching a bonfire of books. An Inquisition feel, a Kristalnacht feel about it. Next chapter is inevitably the burning of the witch, or the gas chamber. I poked about in the edge of the Mayo conflagration. Picked up two books. "Can I have these?" He shrugged. I have them. One is *Leabhuir an tSean Tioma*, by William Bedel, the Irish language bible published in 1827. And the other is the Irish dictionary written by Thaddeus Connellan, published in 1821. Rare enough. Myself and the library of TCD appear to have the only two copies in Ireland. No wonder I suppose, the rest probably burnt by guys clearing their attics.

So I don't knock suburban folks…who buy books. It's a bread and butter issue. Though another reason for not knocking suburbs is that it's really quite rude and offensive and dismissive. Being dismissive of large swathes of humanity is ridiculous, just arrogance really. Believe you me, as one who has spent a large part of his life being rude and offensive and arrogant I know of what I write. But none of that knowledge helps me to say anything interesting or enlightening about the route between Johnstown Avenue and Flower Grove.

We'll have to do with a few lines of mumbling anecdotage.

When I was a very little boy that roundabout was a country crossroads. The Beechwood Hotel stood mouldering here at the junction. And Ballinclea road itself was little more than a winding country lane. A lane infested with bats, I've no idea why. Perhaps the old barns and outhouses of Ballinclea House and Belton's farm gave them roosting room. But certainly when cycling along here in the evening they swooped at us like spitfires in the Battle of Britain. Something like that. Or maybe not at all like that. Maybe I just had a poster of spitfires on my bedroom wall.

Avondale was mostly Belton's farms. Dick Belton was a golf club friend of my father. An alcoholic, he spent most of his life selling off land for development and drinking the proceeds in Killiney Golf Club. Snipes of champagne, he drank, morning to night. Then went home to *Bellevue House*. Decided to sell it to the nuns. Cluny Convent now. "But where will we live" asked his little daughter Avril. Or something along those lines. "Don't you worry dear" was his reply, "I'm building a big bungalow on Ballinclea Road". Which he did. And all was happy. Little Avril went to Holy Child Convent with my sisters. And

another pupil there was little Elizabeth O'Driscoll. And they all grew up, as little girls always do. Unless they die like my daughter. And little Avril became Avril Doyle, Fine Gael MEP. And little Elizabeth became Liz McManus, Labour TD.

Goes to show, you just can't keep a Holy Child girl down.

Move on, let the readers write their own jokes about that remark.

I move on, backwards and forwards between Johnstown Avenue and Flower Grove, carrying out my extensive field research. Then, via Rochestown Avenue and Bakers Corner and places like that I drove to my

place in Mayo. I had told myself I'd have another bash there, a final attempt to write this piece. I sat in front of the computer. I read more or less the entire edition of the online *Guardian* newspaper. In the old days writers

used to pare pencils, to put off the evil. Nowadays we read newspapers online. And carry on inappropriate intimate email relationships with women in Australia, that sort of thing. But the Guardian was read and Susan my cyber mistress was not on line, and there was nothing for it. Except to face the truth. There's nothing really to say about the area between Johnstown Road and Flower Grove. There wasn't then when I

lived there, and there isn't now. Still too new, I suppose, I'm an historian and like to get a hang on old stuff. And if I can't do that I lapse into tittle tattle. So leave it there.

39 FLOWER GROVE, GLENAGEARY

THE FIRST SEMI DETACHED houses I ever saw were those being built up along Killiney Road opposite the house of my parents. I was very small. I'd never seen a semi detached house. I got confused. I understood houses, separate houses. We lived in a house. And I understood terraces. My great uncle lived in a terrace, Dungar Terrace in Dún Laoghaire. He had a statue of the Sacred Heart on the half landing, glowing red votive light and all. Throbbing heart on exterior of chest. You had to be there. But it was a terrace, understandable. And I understood flats. My Granny lived in a flat in Longford Terrace in Monkstown. She'd been married very young, to a much older man. And had been about forty years a widow. I reckon this gave her a lot of time to think. And she hadn't come to cheerful conclusions. She lived up gloomy stairs. A woman of great age and solemnity, sitting there all in black. You didn't want to be there. But nonetheless it was a flat. An understandable sort of living space.

I just didn't get semis. Aged five or so looking across the road at the new semis going up I just... didn't... get them. My father explained. That's really two houses, joined in the middle. It was like he was telling me the facts of life. Which, now that I remember, he actually never did. Not from reticence I'm sure. He couldn't be bothered. I reckon he felt that explaining semi detached houses was going more or less far enough, parental input wise.

I studied architecture in UCD and it didn't help at all. I still didn't get semis. But I sure as hell got them when we moved into Flower Grove. It wasn't great. A strange oppressive feel to the location. A sort of closed in feeling, like a village where everyone had married their cousins for generations. But of course they hadn't. A new enough road, people were strangers to each other, and had settled there from all over. It's probably only now, now that the trees have matured and a new generation is coming along that they're getting round to marrying their cousins.

It was around this time and location that H's publishing career lifted off. She had started as a secretarial sort of person to a religious publishing company. Yes, a religious one. Anyone have a problem with that? Anyone flipping back bemused to my pages on life in Adelaide Street? Forget it. The Lord prefers one reformed sinner than a hundred who've never been in a three in a bed sex romp in their life.

Off she flew. Onwards and upwards. One minute she was in her husband's bed, and the next in Frankfurt and Chicago and New York with the likes of Liam Millar, Seán Ó Boyle, Michael Adams, Michael Gill, Michael O'Brien. A lot of Michaels in the Irish publishing business. And several of them should really have had the surname Mouse. But who am I to talk. H became the administrator of the trade organisation of the Irish book publishing industry. This was a high flying high profile job. She worked late. And sometimes came home a bit befuddled from functions. On one of which occasions, I distinctly recall, a husband does…she climbed fragrantly into the bed…much of the fragrance alcohol, but attractive nonetheless. I touched her gently on the shoulder. A husband does. She said "oh stop it for godsakes X." And shrugged my hand away and turned her back and went to sleep. X, I thought, X ? Her boss was an X. I pondered for awhile. And decided it wasn't really worth pondering. If she had instead said go for it X I would certainly have thought about the matter long and hard. And strongly advised her to ask X for a significant pay rise in the morning.

Financially though we were already on the pig's back. Well, she was. I was broke. And my poverty sort of dragged her down to my level. So we were both broke again pretty soon. Give us a job, I said to her. She did. This involved me, Liam Millar, and an estate car loaded down with books driving across to the UK, across the UK, and thence to Frankfurt. Liam Millar didn't fly. Or drive. I have never liked flying, but like driving. Liam Millar had to be gotten to Frankfurt. The books had to be gotten to Frankfurt. It was a marriage made in heaven.

Liam was the founder of The Dolmen Press, grand old man of Irish publishing. He was a fine man and a great publisher. Terrible businessman and an almighty drinker. And a religious maniac to boot. I liked him enormously. It was a great trip. Drink? Involved. Though as I was driving I was a mere observer. Mostly. And a sight it was to see. We crossed the Irish Sea by ferry, drinking. And then down across the UK, drinking. Though one non drinking stop was in Coventry where Liam wanted to show me some details of the cathedral. Epstein's St Michael. Just like the one in my own Dún Laoghaire church. Well, sort of. And the Graham Sutherland. And the screen of saints and angels. Yes of course I knew all this, but not through the eyes of a Liam Millar. It makes a difference, whose eyes are leading the way. And of course in Coventry I didn't know the pub he liked. But I know it now. And so onward to Dover. And Calais. And thence Bruges. And on and on to Frankfurt.

And much the same coming home.

Flower Grove to Glenalua Road

BORN IN KILLINEY with, if not a silver spoon, a Killiney accent in my mouth, I decided to move up the hill a bit. I'm not really a swamp sort of person. And yes, I know Flower Grove is higher than, say, Monkstown Farm, both socially and geographically, but it is still a bit of a low lying swamp. And not nearly as high as the top of Killiney Hill. I wanted to be on the top of Killiney Hill. And I suppose I wanted to show my Portlaoise born partner what the world looked like when it didn't look like Laois. It's a duty that, really, for a husband. Particularly with a younger wife. To sort of bring her on a bit, educate, show her new horizons. I have always taken that duty seriously. And, as a consequence, she has always thought me a right royal and patronising pain in the arse.

Flower Grove was in fact the sort of place that people would leave after a few years. That, or stay there forever. Frank Delaney left. He had lived across the road from us. Who he, the readers query? And of course that question is the answer. But for the record he was a plummy voiced media man about books, and he soon put Flower Grove behind him. Went to England, got plummier. And Michael Ó Nualláin, he had lived in Flower Grove too, and left. And went to live in Monkstown's Belgrave Square. The brother of Flann O Brian, he was last heard of campaigning against the erection of Dublin's spire. Lost that battle. Bit of a downer really, being the brother of a famous writer. One must feel the clutching fingers of posterity passing one by.

We set off for the new horizons.

God did it feel good. We were getting out of Flower Grove and had a lovely house awaiting. While not quite rich beyond avarice, we were reasonably well off. Thanks to H's job. I suppose she was lucky in that she had a resident unpaid baby and child minder, a housekeeper, and a cook. I think she called him her husband. With added information of 'he's given up architecture and is writing a book'. And no doubt the people she said this to thought 'he's a useless gobshite, doesn't deserve a wife like her'. Not that they'd say anything like that to her. She'd kill. Intensely loyal, and though she thought me a royal and patronising pain in her arse, she also thought the sun shone out of mine.

A complex relationship.

We brought the complex relationship up to Killiney with our baggages and child. Out of the warrens and burrows of hidden lives and into Avondale Road. Strange that I didn't know anyone on that whole road. Except my ex bank manager, and he I was trying to avoid anyway. We actually hadn't been on the best of terms since he took H and I to the High Court. Yes, the High, no lowly District for our financial affairs. And there in the High he lost his case. I recall the exact moment he lost. He was giving evidence, nonchalantly. He said "well actually I found them personally rather amusing", referring to H and I. I knew it was the wrong thing to say. It made him sound like a jerk. He was a jerk. But not good to show it off in public. I looked at Judge Costello and saw the verdict on his face. He was thinking this bank manager guy is a royal and patronising pain in the arse.

So up yours Ulster Bank, I hear you've gone bust since.

But it is strange, a huge long road like Avondale, and me not knowing anyone on it. My parents had lived on the huge long Killiney Road, and, while they may not have talked much to anyone, they certainly knew everyone for a mile in each direction. And what they had for breakfast. I suppose times had changed. Lives lived in warrens are lived in deeper burrows now. But now these days they've changed a little more, because now I do know someone on Avondale Road. My long lost cousin Peter Fisher. In number one one six. And he was there all along. But, being long lost, I didn't know.

We cross over Avondale and out into Ballinclea. And head left towards the entrance to Cluny School. But don't go in, particularly if you're a middleaged man. Not that they bother me, schoolgirls. I never look at women younger than my older daughter. It's a sort of rule of thumb, and saves a man from looking ridiculous or ending up on a sex register, or both. And my older daughter is twenty seven. Getting older by a year each year. And thus the women I can look at also get older by a year each year. As I in turn get older by a year. It works very well as a system. But of course would completely break down if your older daughter were only twelve.

Along Ballinclea, past the house where Tom Day now a bigshot in Lisney's was a childhood friend. Past the triangle where my father would go down every evening to post letters to his employers. He called it 'the firm'. A cigarette salesman, he went round shops collecting orders. Posted them in every evening. No email in those days. His letterbox still there, buried in the wall. But my father's hand will never touch that iron slot again, It's not a hand no more. It's just a complexity of little bones. Like you'd see in an illustration proving the descent of man from monkey. A tangle of little bones, buried in Deans Grange. On the protestant side of the cemetery. Dead right. A man wouldn't want to rot among catholics. Or vice versa, of course.

So onwards, up Killiney Road and past the house where I was born.

I glance along the garden walls and I see two trees planted there in the back. One a palm tree, a cordyline, my mother brought it yonks ago from her father's mansion in Dalkey. And the other a pine. I remember my mother getting that. We were on a picnic up the Dublin mountains. She came grinning along the road back to the car, swinging a little baby tree she'd pulled up out of the plantation. She was strange, that mother of mine. Lived in Italy as a girl in the nineteen thirties. Among fascists and titled folks. I have photos of her quite beautiful. But she came back to Ireland and married a protestant cigarette salesman. And her life became grey, and silent, in a silent house.

But shit, I suppose she got free cigarettes.

God I'm a flippant bugger, walking on. Up to the castle, Killiney Castle, turn sharp right and on up the hill. Past protestant church and catholic church, opposite each other like those in Monkstown. It's only in long established areas that the factions look across at each other in this way. In Dublin's newer sprawling areas there are new catholic churches sure, but no protestants looking at them over the wall.

Past the entrance to Killiney Hill. Victoria Park that was. That sculpture to be seen through the gates is *Thus Daedalus Flew*. It dates from 1986 and I suppose it's not bad. As Dún Laoghaire public sculpture goes. And it's great for kids to climb on, and their climbing keeps the bronze wings polished.

Opposite here there's a house by the name of *Knockaderry*. Like the letterbox down at the triangle, this house always reminds me of my father.

It's a literary matter. Not that my father had any literary pretensions, I don't think he ever read a complete book in his life. But he does have one claim for residence in the literary pantheon. He ran over and killed Seán Ó Faoileán's dog outside this house. The short story writer rushed out of the gates in bits and made a complete ten volume saga out of the event. With index and end notes and full critical analysis thrown in.

So they did their thing, stoic apologising motorist, hysterical victim, and dead dog. Neither the motorist nor victim (the dog didn't care) knew that they had another connection. Because yes, they did have a more intimate connection, so to speak. They felt they only had the corpse of a dead dog between them. They had nothing in common at all. My father not only did not read books, he strongly disliked people who read books, or anyone of the artistic or cultural persuasion. Which more or less put me his only son into a certain bracket in his affections.

The connection... the fact is that Seán Ó Faoileán the noted short story writer and onetime dog owner was very friendly with an Englishwoman by the name of Maud Cooke. No harm in that. If a short story writer can't have an affair with an Englishwoman of any name then it's a pretty damn kettle of fish indeed. Things have come to a pretty pass. But they haven't. And they did, have the affair. And she wasn't a bad looking English woman either. I know, I have the photos. And the connection between this English woman and my father and Seán Ó Faoileán? Triangular. The English woman was the estranged wife of my father's cousin, Brien Kennedy. A designer of boats. I knew him in his old age, and I in fact edited his autobiography for him. It was my job. But it was also my job to listen to old boys talking about their lives. And Brien talked. And told me. Maud and Seán were an item, once.

Why would he lie? Granted, if H had an affair with an Irish short story writer I mightn't let it be known. I'd actually hush it up a bit. The embarassment factor. I'd prefer her affairs to be with guys who can write a full length book. And I'm sure she would too. Something about a short story writer in bed worries me, from the female side of things. One gets the  impression that he might be in a rush to get things over with. That sort of impression. Whereas the full length bloke, he who gets involved in major work of epic proportions... well... he would, I feel, somehow... be... more... you know.

But that's all literary fiddle faddle. Brien Kennedy was a technical man, a naval architect. He wouldn't have known a short story from ... he just wasn't a man of books and didn't give a monkey's what sort of stuff O'Faoileán wrote. Seán was just a writer. In that house. Had an affair with Maud. Good luck to them. Brien was already with Christine at that stage. Life moves on. It hardly matters.

So why tell it now? Because it matters to me, that connection. There's a pattern somewhere there. My father driving his car. Dog runnning out of the gate. Owner following. Death. Relationships and hidden love affairs. A pattern. I can see it. And if the reader can't then I'm not quite as good a writer as I think.

Maybe I should try short stories.

Whatever, whatever about the maybes.

There's also certainties. Certainly here I should turn up Glenalua Road, up behind Killiney Village, up right again to our new house. And our new life. The folks who live on the hill.

MORRIGAN BOOKS

H HAD LONG BEEN INVOLVED in the book publishing business. Rising from lowly humble typist answering phones to mysterious positions where she seemed to spend an inordinate amount of time at book launches and functions and book fairs in Ireland and abroad. In Ireland I would troll along to some of these business events with her, mainly for the free wine and to see if there were any interesting women. The wine was glunk and the chances of finding interesting women in Irish book publishing were and are extremely remote. I already had the most interesting woman in the industry so I fell back on the wine and nibbles and observing. It didn't take long to realise that a fair proportion of Irish book publishers consisted of a medley of dullards, fantasists and incompetents. In short, a fair representation of Irish society generally.

I decided I could do better. I couldn't. But didn't know that yet, so H and I started our own publishing business. For reasons of certain magic and occult interests of the time, we called it Morrigan. After the Irish Goddess of darkness. An elemental force, she is prone to shape changing. Sometimes appearing as a young seductive woman. At others as a shrieking crone. And in between times hanging around disguised as a black and sinister bird. Not sure if our logo above got across that message. But that's probably just as well because, apart from *The Occult Directory* (don't even ask) Morrigan did not publish magic, of black or white or any colour intervening. It was very establishment. And the first book, *The Guide To Dublin Schools*, was, disastrously, number one in the best seller list for months. That unfortunate success encouraged us to publish a lot more books. Which generally meant a lifetime of living in hope and losing lots of money. It took a long while of wandering round the south side to see sense. Now in this new century we still tick it over. Less is more in the publishing business. Our *Diaries of Mary Hayden* comes along in five volumes and run to 2360 pages. Not for the DART or the LUAS. Made a bomb. And not sold in Irish bookshops either. This is the type of thing that sells to major world libraries and universities and American academia. In publishing terms, myself and H are, finally, posh. Who'd have thunk, as the saying says.

THE COACH HOUSE, KILLINEY VILLAGE

THERE WAS UNTIL recent years a shopkeeping family in Dún Laoghaire, the McGoverns. Vegetable shops and knick knack shops and grocery shops, all down around the People's Park end of the town. In my childhood days they also had nurseries up near the triangle at Ballinclea Road. My father bought tomato plants there. My mother planted them. We ate them. Until they were all gone. Tomatoes, for weeks on end. They'll go off, my mother said. Eat up. Tomatoes are very good for you. I've no idea whether they're very good for you or not. And I'm sure my mother didn't either. But they were there, free, outside the window. Saved on the housekeeping. My mother got a thing from my father called 'the housekeeping'. It was never enough. She said that a lot. Sometimes she emphasised this by throwing plates at his head and storming out of the room.

They say a man always marries a woman like his mother. In some ways I did too. H never had enough 'housekeeping'. Most of what she had she actually had to earn herself. I am a poet. We poets are poor people. She appreciates that, but has often thrown things at me to emphasise her general problem. Cups. Bottles. Glasses. Chickens. Whole cooked roast dinners. Following which she would storm, out. This happened a lot in Adelaide Street. Though that probably wasn't about housekeeping. Perhaps more about the sleeping arrangements in number thirty-one. Whatever. I would catch up with her somewhere near the St Nicholas Montessori School. And caveman-like drag her back screaming and roaring to the slum. No-one really noticed. People in Adelaide Street minded their own business.

Living in Adelaide Street we actually shopped in McGovern's shop, more or less around the corner. H would buy vegetables there, either to throw at me or to cook a meal, depending on how the relationship was panning out at any given time. I knew the McGoverns, the children of the shopkeepers. As a teenager some of the best fights of my life involved these guys. They were volatile. But one of them wasn't, one was calm, and I hadn't actually known him as a teenager. He was steady, respectable. And what would I want to be mixing in those circles for?

Jimmy McGovern, he owned *The Coachhouse* in Killiney.

We rented it from him. There was no choice. We had to move. It was either die of despair in Flower Grove, or move. Well there was one other choice. Go mad. But this would have involved one of those depressing court cases beloved of *The Irish Times* and *Sunday Indo*, where one half of a south county Dublin middleclass couple…must be a south county Dublin middleclass couple… does the other half to death. Either myself or H would've gone mad, and done for the other. Just because of the architecture in Flower Grove. Architecture is extraordinarily influential. It is actually quite unnatural for a man to kill his wife, unless of course he is an Afghan. There he'll kill her at the drop of a burkah. Or the drop of a hint that she's learning to read. But that's…a different world. Round these parts people go mad from semi detached houses. And do unnatural and irrational things. God knows what will happen in Kabul if they start building semis.

Myself and H arranged with Jimmy McGovern to collect the keys at *The Coachhouse* from the previous tenant. She'd be waiting for us. She was. She was Mary Bourke Kennedy. I knew her. Still blonde, still speaking with that attractive lisp, still Mary Finnegan.

I had known her as a schoolgirl of Cluny Convent. Not in the biblical sense, to my teenage regret, but we were quite friendly. Just teenagers mucking around the place. Avondale Road was only being built then, and I would be down there a lot at the sites, stealing wood for my canoe building business. This I had started at the age fifteen, and it was very successful. No doubt because, as Harvard Business School will confirm, the best place to start a manufacturing business is right beside a source of free raw materials.

Cluny School schoolgirls were thick on the ground around Avondale Road in those days. There were still fields there and lanes and a summery sort of old fashioned feeling to the times. Butterflies, hedgerows, birdsong. And Mary Finnegan on her bicycle with her blonde hair flying and her blue Cluny skirts around her suntanned legs was…well…you get the picture. A picture waiting for John Betjeman to write, William Leech to paint. It was strange, meeting her in the Coach House circumstances after so many years. And so I got to know her again, after all these years. That was equally strange.

Jimmy McGovern died of cancer not long after he had rented us that house. And years before that, one of those teenage boys who used hang round the Cluny girls, my mate Brian Francis, he died of heroin. Deaths occur at random times, for different reasons. But strangely sometimes different deaths seem to belong to the same story, as if the death exists in a timeless place. Much like love. And love affairs too, I suppose.

Marriages, unlike love, do not exist in a timeless place. They ebb and they flow. Milly had now left her husband or he left her. In any event she set up her own home. I don't think this was anything to do with me. But I certainly suffered for it. Ferociously intelligent and astute, with the arrogance that went with it, she maintained a calm and cold exterior to the world.

But of course intelligent and astute and calm and cold women are the same as the rest of us. They hit the emotional buffers now and then. When Milly hit the emotional buffers she hit them big time. She would take to her bed, weeping. I would be summoned. I would clean her flat. Feed her little son. Force her to get up out of the bed, wash her, dress her. And she would re emerge into the world. And walk calmly and coldly and beautiful down the Monkstown Road. You crossed her at your peril.

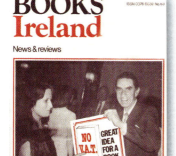

H campaigning on cover of Books Ireland, with British colleague.

Unfortunately lots of times when she walked calmly and coldly and beautiful down the Monkstown Road she also walked calmly and coldly and beautiful through the door of Goggins Pub. And then late at night my phone would ring and H would wake beside me in the bed and say 'it's Milly'. And it was. And H depending on her mood would say 'well she's your girlfriend not mine' and turn and go back to sleep or alternatively sit up and issue orders. Get up and dress and go out into the night and look to Milly. But it made no difference what her attitude was because I had to go anyway. There was what the Irish ancients called a geis on me, an obligation. There are no external penalties for those who break a geis. It's just a part of him. Breaking a geis is just like cutting off a hand. It changes a person. He's no longer who he is.

So I'd leave H snug in her nice warm bed and go out into the miserable cold empty streets of Dún Laoghaire at one o'clock in the bloody morning. It always seemed to be one o'clock in the morning. And there would be Milly sitting on her doorstep like a child. She wouldn't want to go in. And I couldn't take her home because by that time we'd all of us moved along from the three in a bed sex romp aspect of life's rich tapestry, so I'd have to sit there beside her and talk. And eventually she'd give me her doorkey and I'd open the door and help her up and help her in and help her up the stairs.

H was working full time now. She ran an office in Dublin and always seemed to be hopping off to book fairs and the like. Chicago. New York. London. Frankfurt. I was the new man house husband, bringing up the children. Single handed. Though when she came home in the evenings she would lend a hand. Washing clothes and tidying the house and ironing and cooking meals for the next day. Little stuff like that. It was useful. And she was useful also in keeping me in touch with the outside world. A bloke bringing up children on top of Killiney Hill can

H with Michael Adams (died 2009), founder of Irish Academic Press.

get a bit isolated, inward looking. News of Irish bookish events, which I'd given up going to for mental health reasons. And news from abroad. Yes H would do her best to keep me in touch with important goings on in the Irish and international book publishing scene.

"Well", she says to me, back from Frankfurt once, "so and so is impotent". So and so being a leading Irish publisher of the time. His name appears nowhere in this book. So all you other guys relax. If that's the correct word. In the context.

"How do you know?" I ask, the obvious question from any husband.

"So and so slept with him in Frankfurt".

"Ah", says I. I knew so and so. A British publishing apparachik, she and (one of) her boyfriends had stayed with us onetime. In gratitude she gave us a ceramic wall plaque depicting a happy smiling sun. And he brought the gift of a book. About Scottish dialects. Lowland Scottish dialects.

"So and so slept with so and so in Frankfurt and in the morning she told you he was impotent?"

"At breakfast".

"Ah. But surely if a woman sleeps with a man on a business trip she might at least have breakfast with him, not her mates".

"Not so and so. If the guy is impotent".

"So what you're telling me is this. You women sit there at breakfast at book fairs, stuffing your faces with croissants and maple syrup pancakes, discussing the sexual goings on…

cLé

HILARY KENNEDY
Administrator

The Irish Book Publishers' Association
Cumann Leabhar Fhoilsitheoiri Eireann Teo
The Writers' Centre, 19 Parnell Square, Dublin 1.
Telephone: 872 9090   *Fax:* 872 2035

or lack of them...of the night before?"

"You want we should talk about books?"

The photo of H and myself here was not, despite appearances, taken with the background of Killiney hills. Rather it is in Kerry. Around this time we went to visit my aunt. I liked my aunt. I'd been good friends with her in London years before. She was a chain smoking nurse of a certain age with seductive knowing eyes. I like chain smoking women of a certain age with seductive knowing eyes, aunt or not. Twenty five years older than me or not. At one stage she and I evolved a plan to go to Yugoslavia together. The world is probably not ready for further details of this arrangment. But it's OK. Because I went somewhere else instead. Oh well. *Non, je ne regrette rien*. As my aunt would have sung. If she had been French. She wasn't. She was a retired Irish nurse living in Kerry and we went to visit. The visit changed our life. Property ladder wise. Read on.

GONE TO CANADA

ANOTHER BREAK OUT from the south side. H took a break from her job and we went to live in Canada for awhile. And while there went to visit our old home town of Glastonbury Connecticut. To remember, those times. And particularly the baby we lost there. The photo above shows H at the swimming hole, the year after we married. She's sitting down because she's heavily pregnant with Siobhan. Parked nearby was our old Ford car.

And the other photo? Twenty years later. Same H, same swimming hole. The wood of the seat has rotted away some. Things change. H is a calm mature woman now, and not a pregnant girl anymore. And another thing different too. Because parked right there now was the open topped white Cadillac we'd arrived in. Vulgar? You bet. The only way to go back to a town where you had tough times. It's the American way.

NARIN, HOLMSTON AVENUE, GLENAGEARY

BACK FROM CANADA we were sucking diesel. Us installed in a nice house and a beautiful Au Pair installed alongside us. Here she is on that Glenageary gravel. Valerie. She's a doctor in France now. And we're all feeling better already.

I was running an architectural business and was involved in publishing. H was on a upward trajectory in her own seperate book publishing work. We had a fair bit of money. Though perhaps rather less than we thought. The electricity did get turned off now and again. And the gas. And the car was repossessed. But we got another pretty quickly. And Valerie went back to Paris. But we got another pretty quickly. Babette. From Lyons. Nowhere near as beautiful as Valerie. But more interesting. A small plain girl…maybe H picked her…she eventually went back to Lyons and became a postwoman.

We went to Canada again around this time. H was doing a trade fair in Chicago. I flew over to New York with our small child. Met up with H in Toronto. Not quite sure what we did there. Stayed quite some time. But I definitely bought a hat. And, on return, put it on my head and went up the Sugarloaf.

Our first baby had died in America. And H herself nearly died giving birth to our third. It was in Mount Carmel in Churchtown. We obviously had more money than medical judgement. But to be fair, it was a condition. They just didn't know how to deal with it. I waited outside the delivery room. I don't do being present at births. I'm a primitive sort of person. I think all that is a woman thing. I don't really approve of male gynaecologists either. What's wrong with a man that he wants to spend his life wearing rubber gloves in female innards? There's got to be some psychiatric explanation. How can he deal with his own women after coming home from work? I think I know a fair bit about sex, and I certainly know that the more mysterious and unspoken it remains the better. No, women should keep childbirth as a woman thing. Women midwives, women gynacologists, everyone involved. There's tribes where women speak a different language than the men. I like that, seems the way to go. I like my women to be strange, and different, and apart somehow. Which is probably just as well, because most of them are.

But I also like them to be alive.

H nearly died in Mount Carmel. I knew she was dying when doctors rushed in and out avoiding me. I'm pretty quick that way. It was placenta accreta. You don't want to know. Particularly if you're a man. There's a lot of blood involved. But they patched her up. I went home to sleep, and to mind the child we already had there. In the middle of the night I had a phone call from a friend. Neasa. She phoned me to tell me that her husband had died that very night, in St Michael's in Dún Laoghaire. He was very young, a heavy drinker. I liked him very much. David O'Hare. A professional photographer, he had taken photos of me for some publicity thing. That's how I'd met him and Neasa. And now she had phoned me up in the middle of the night to say he was dead.

As she told me I remembered kissing her, somewhere. Drink? Involved. And how she tut tutted, about her husband being right over there. And how I had said I don't believe in kissing my friends' wives behind their backs. Glib, I suppose, but probably an appropriate dictum. I remembered all that, putting down the phone in the quiet house. Child asleep. Au pair asleep. H very ill in hospital. And I thought well, Dave won't be watching, next time I kiss her. But I never did again, not really, not that way anyway. Kissed her at the funeral yes. But that's a different sort of kiss.

Mount Carmel sent H home after a week. But she was dying with an infection and, barely home, she haemorraged again. Rushed in a blood swamped ambulance to Holles Street. I more or less said goodbye as they carried her in. Because I thought she was more or less about dead.

She was. It was the worst of time. I'd always known I'd always loved her more than anyone or anything. So I didn't get that oh I love her and now she's going to die thing. I just got the knowing, this is the worst of time.

She lost practically all her blood, going in one end and out the other. She was very ill and in hospital for quite awhile. I am a Christian, of the candle lighting faction. So I lit candles for her, and did a deal with God. He kept his side of the bargain. I started working on mine.

Holmston Avenue to Sandycove Avenue North

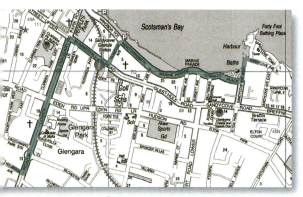

NO-ONE COULD CALL the Lower Glenageary Road interesting. It has the feel of a gulch, the feel of a canyon, the feel of a route for the 7A bus. Above us the cliffs of the backs of squares and on the other side the front gardens of very uninteresting looking houses. Reminds me strongly of coming into Euston Station on the train from Holyhead. Those high backs of houses with their stuck on bathrooms where, or so John Betjeman wrote, lonely business girls had baths. I was always an admirer of Betjeman, not to mention of business girls in baths. The lonelier the better. This admiration, of the poet, led me into all sorts of abuse from my intellectual superiors. Back in the Bamboo Coffee Bar. They seemed to prefer Elliot. Uh huh. Who was to know then that in 2008 I would win the Scottish Blue Butterfly poetry award? Christian poetry award. Yep, so there. 2008. Big poetical year. Same year I was expelled from *Poetry Ireland* for political incorrectness.

Some time way in the past this uninteresting Lower Glenageary Road linked the two ancient routes of Eden-Corrig-Tivoli to that of Upper Glenageary. It gave access to the Glen of The Sheep, from which the area takes its name. That glen was centred on what is or was until recently known as Swan's Hollow. After a Mr Swan rather than some Mr and Mrs Birds. That's the dip in the road after Rathdown School, the old Hillcourt House of 1830. The interior of which, I have read, is decorated with a painted frieze depicting 'idealized rural scenes and arcadian landscapes'. I haven't actually seen this frieze myself, having stayed well away from Rathdown since, as mentioned earlier, I was arrested there as a teenager.

It's a long way from rural scenes and arcadian landscapes that we are now. But we do have a view of the sea in front of us down the hill. A view of the sea lets some kind of air into the soul. I can't really stay very far from the sea. Though I do plan on being buried in Roscommon. That is for different reasons, occult matters. And I won't be needing a good view then. My soul will be well free in the air.

The crossroads where we pass over the Corrig-Eden roads is precisely where once was the little village of Kilnagashaugh. There are stones of an old church beneath our feet. And the graves of holy men and women. What price those prayers now, one wonders? One wonders about a lot of things. Why precisely did we move from Glenageary to Sandycove? It is not entirely clear. Restlessness perhaps. And also I think, as I seem to remember, the landlady was a pain in the neck. They have that quality anyway. It's no way to build a relationship, the landlady tenant thing. Goes against the Irish grain. There's a glitch in our DNA, scientists call it eviction. My friend Michael who had known that particular landlady as a teenager informed me that she was remarkable, among that teenage cohort, for certain physical characteristics. Unfortunately this information, apart from being far too much, was of absolute no use to me. And joins an encyclopaedia of useless information that the same Michael has imparted over the years. But he did work in advertising. And it's an urge. To communicate. Whatever the cost or the effect on the sanity of the communicatee.

But anyway, for whatever reason, move we did.

The hippie type VW camper van had not survived. It never took us to Italy and places sunny. We wouldn't get to go there for another twenty years. And then by Ryanair. The building business had done for the van. I'd had to dismantle all the fitting out of bunks and the little fold down table where we would have eaten *petto di vitello arrotolato* and sipped our *granita di caff`e* and drank our wine in the hills above Arma di Taggia. Yes, I had to sadly take apart all those fittings, not to mention all those plans and dreams. To carry concrete blocks and sewer pipes and the like to house extensions in Mount Merrion.

Yes, my beloved camper van was long scrapped now. It had become a wreck. Shelley had a poem for my feelings. Shelley has a poem for lots of my feelings. *Look on my works, ye mighty and despair. Nothing beside remains. Round the decay of that colossal wreck, boundless and bare, the lone and level sands stretch far away.* More or less sums it up. How come Heaney hasn't got a poem like that? Or a poem for anyone's feelings? That fellow can't really write. How come we can't face up to these facts? Sign of maturity, facing reality.

Whatever. H and I now had an estate car sort of vehicle. And in this we ferrried our belongings and our couple of small children down to the new house. It was all a bit fraught. H was lucky to be alive. And I would watch her carefully, obsessively, just to make sure she was still ticking over. Was that the right colour in her face? You're looking very pale, sit down. That sort of remark. As things turned out I should have been looking out for myself. Yes the reaper is always hovering round. But it transpired that he'd moved on from H. And had his eye on me. Grimly.

Let's write of other things.

Iris Murdoch for a start. She was 'prone to sleep with anyone', said the English critic A.N. Wilson. And he should know. He knows most things about literature, and literateurs. But what he probably doesn't know is that there was, here at the crossroads at the bottom of Lower Glenageary Road, a large hardware and household shop. Murdochs. The building is still there, red brick, vaguely anonymous these days, of indeterminate function. High up on the gable there was once a sign that read 'Pink Paraffin'. A bloke misses that.

Dame Iris was connected to this family, she herself having been born in Dublin's Blessington Street. Born to, by strange coincidence, a family with its roots in the sheep business. Strange coincidence? Yes, remember, we have just come down from the Glen of The Sheep. It all ties together. Thankfully. Because in 2009 I was to earn big bucks from *The Irish Times* writing my column *Connections* on such strange coincidental matters.

Iris Murdoch. Sad really. Little girl in Blessington Street. Goes to England. Writes novels. Has lots of sex. Gets Alzheimers. Dies. Forgotten. Very sad in fact, particularly as while typing away, I realise that apart from the little girl in Blessington Street bit, I could be sketching in my own life story.

Move along quickly.

Something Stalinist about the name *The People's Park*. A vaguely North Korean ring to that. But then, one supposes, Victorian British culture was quite totalitarian. Though startlingly efficient. Whereas Stalinism only succeeded in transforming a bunch of peasants into a nation of gangsters and an incredible number of loose and tarty looking women. Most seemingly putting themselves through university by working as hookers. A good rule of thumb is to avoid any woman whose name ends in *ova*. In contrast to all that the British version of totalitarianism built excellent drains and waterworks… and parks.

Once a quarry, this park is actually a very nice place to be. When the autumn of my days arrive, if I survive this late summer, I shall be spotted there betimes, brooding on it all. I shall be an old man in a park. Far too old for the young mothers at the playground to worry if I am a paedophile lurking, just… old.   Not a bother to anyone. An old man in a park. The role appeals. And if I am blind as well as old I shall get my carer to lead me to the garden of smelly plants laid out here for the blind. And I'll walk around them sniffing, remembering how they looked. Flowers and plants and pretty things and pretty girls and lovely places. Yes I'll do that, when I'm very old.

But I'm not there yet.

I'm walking down Summerhill, moving house, again. A lovely name, summerhill, and I don't know where it comes from. And maybe should look it up for the readers here. But I couldn't be arsed, to be honest. In my business I spend more than enough time in libraries and archives. And a writer is, I suppose, in many ways a teacher. And there comes a time when a teacher has to just let people do things for themselves. That'll be their learning. So try google.

Rosmeen Gardens is interesting. Well it is to me. It actually doesn't look that interesting to the people who live there. I never saw such dull and downtrodden looking folks  in my life, the world's worries on their shoulders. And suspicious with it. I wonder why that should be? Probably the site of an atrocity in ancient times, something like that. Places have their own spirits.

It and the adjoining Rosmeen Park are built on the grounds of Granite Hall, one of those twin houses built by Mr Smith the stone merchant for Dún Laoghaire Harbour. The other twin survives in Clarinda, but Granite Hall is gone. But none of that is the reason this place is interesting.

During the war my father was trundling along here in a tram. Living in Blackrock, he was on his way to see my mother in Dalkey. These were their courting days. Suddenly (he told me, many times), suddenly there was a very large explosion right in front of the tram. The tram stopped. It was a bomb, a German bomb from a german bomber overhead. Historians suspect that they weren't trying to get my father, no, but that they were interested in the mailboat nearby. The mailboat that was bringing thousands of Irish over to the UK to join the forces there. Whatever about all that, the bomb landed on the corner of Rosmeen Gardens and missed my father in his tram. If…if that bomb had hit that tram…who would I be? I often wonder that, and what book would I be writing?

It's hard to tell.

Perhaps that bomb did hit that tram, and all that followed is illusion.

Perhaps. There are many dimensions. Many avenues to reality. And, indeed, many avenues here, avenues of the physical variety, leading down to the seafront on our left. Martello, that remembers the tower that once stood nearby. But that's a dead end so no use going down there. Unless one wants to see the house where the woman who invented the Lyons Tea minstrels once lived. Those little unpolitically correct blacked up guys on the tea packets. Buy Lyons Tea, diddle diddle dee. All that. Remember? No?

Oh alright. We'll go down Islington Avenue. Reminds me of my old mate George Potter, this place. An American artist, portly and courtly he promenades his adopted town, and paints it well. And I have his *Islington Avenue* on my wall. Well, a copy of the painting. He is an RHA.

Many years ago the restaurant at the bottom here used be the Chatterbox Coffee Bar. A sort of branch office of the Bamboo Coffee Bar. If one got bored in one the other was only a short stroll away. The conversation would be precisely the same, but the ambiance different.

Baile Mac Gabhann does not translate as Newtownsmith. But, as my friend John Cully is wont to say, we must always remember what country we woke up in this morning. If it was Ireland, then meaningless road signs mean as much as everything else around us. This is a land of mysticism and wonder.

Newtownsmith takes its name from the builder I mentioned above, George Smith, the contractor who made a fortune supplying stone for the construction of Dún Laoghaire Harbour. Though it does seem that, in fact, his fortune was pretty well assured even before that. This area of County Dublin had been for many years a source of granite. It went far

and wide. Kylemore Abbey on the far west coast of Ireland was built of Dalkey granite. Something like the building of Stonehenge, that effort, lugging great blocks of stone for hundreds of miles.

This area is familiar. We've been this way before. But last time I was a small boy heading to Glasthule Church from nursery school. Now I am a grown man taking my wife to her new home in Sandycove. The harbour lies ahead. Much older than Dún Laoghaire harbour itself, this was built in the 18th century to accommodate barges, stone ferrying barges. These were going back and forth to Dublin city with material for the construction of the South Wall.

And over the harbour the twin curvey profiles of that so called Joyce's Tower alongside Michael Scott's house. As a matter of principle I never write anything about Joyce's Tower. The James Joyce industry petrifies me with boredom. Petrifies. Which means turn to stone. Any more James Joyce stuff and you could use me as a block of stone to build a bloody harbour. Though it must be said…it must be said that H and I did breakfast once on that Bloomsday stuff. At a function. Gizzards and all. And then travel by horse drawn carriage to the tower. Suitably attired, we wore boaters. I actually do have a photo of her wearing nothing but that Bloomsday boater, but that belongs perhaps to a different tale than this.

I often wonder where our boaters went.

Michael Scott who built the curvey house gave me my first job in architecture. I think I was about sixteen. I was the lad on the wrong end of the measuring tape.

Oscaill Cuas an Ghainiml, Thuaidh
SANDYCOVE AVENUE NORTH

My boss, a nineteen year old, he got to hold the end where you read the measurements, and to write them down. Little did I know that one day I would design President Cearbhuill Ó Dálaigh's living room. And garden wall. And the curtain wall of the EBS head office in Westmoreland Street. Not to mention that long brick wall that runs up Appian Way around Fitzwilliam Tennis Club. Perhaps my finest moment. Wall wise.

Little did I know of any of that.

Little did I know a lot.

Islington Avenue
by George Potter RHA

3 SANDYCOVE AVENUE NORTH

THE HOUSE WAS OWNED by Mr Peel. From Northern Ireland. H called him Orange Peel. OK, she was a publishing apparachik, not a script writer. He treated us very well. Which we didn't deserve. We made lousey tenants here. Mostly because we never had any money for the rent. But I did buy a boat, a sailing boat. And parked it here on its trailer on Mr Peel's front drive. Himself and I stood around it, discussing dinghies, sailing, and the sheer exhuberant fun of it all. An immensely courteous man, he didn't once mention the strangeness of the fact that I could afford a boat and not the rent. I'm glad he didn't. It's a difficult concept to get across. That there's boat money and rent money and that the two currencies are not interchangeable. Particularly difficult to get all that across to a Northern Ireland protestant.

Old Mr Peel was too nice to throw us out. So he hired a solicitor who wasn't. An extremely nasty bugger. Centre city office and house in Dalkey. I visited both. Office to negotiate and house to sling a rock through his window. But I saw his wife puttering around in the garden and decided he'd had punishment enough in life. Negotiations in the office failed. It wasn't a good relationship. He reckoned that I was chancing my arm. He was more or less in the right zone there. Takes one to know, etc. Apart from that aspect, I have in fact had very bad luck with solicitors. Or, rather, they have had very bad luck with me. It all seems to go pear shaped for them after falling into my orbit. Though in the case of that Dalkey guy it seems to have gone bad long before. When he married that wife. But time is like that, not necessarily linear. I suspect that it was my curse from the future that mucked up his past.

The first solicitor I ever had threw himself off Dalkey Quarry and was splatted below. Three more were struck off. And two were told by the Law Society to take early retirement. Polite for 'struck off'. And these were the ones who were working on my side. To this day I can't go into a solicitor's office without knowing that the guy is doomed. Blackrock has been a particularly black spot. Hotbed of dodgy solicitors. Two guys there were struck off. And a third was jailed in West Indies for drugs offences. But people will be glad to hear he's still in practice. In Blackrock. It's very strange. Because I actually used pick solicitors out at random, from golden pages or walking past their door. But Man's random is God's plan, I suppose. And these random solicitors are obviously those already heading for doom. I'm merely the harbinger. It's a gift, I suppose.

Around this time I was very ill, on and off. And nearly died. Several times. What I don't know about Dublin hospital intensive care units is not worth knowing. (Try make it to Vincents if you can). It was now H's turn to sit by a sickbed. She did it far better than me. A woman who panics at small events, when something serious kicks in an aura of calm descends. I don't really do calm.

Physical illness was followed by psychiatric. Post traumatic stress disorder. For a couple of years I was out of it. It got so bad I couldn't go out. Couldn't stay in. I took tranquilisers. Lots. I couldn't sleep. I couldn't wake up. I couldn't walk down a street without H. I certainly couldn't go into a shopping centre at all. I couldn't drive in a car by myself. I had to know where H was at all times. In case I needed her. I needed her at all times. If we were walking down the street and she went into a shop I had to be able to see her. If she went out of sight I panicked.

You had to be there. And yes I know many people have been there. And many still are. It's a classic psychiatric condition. The symptoms are standard. But I don't think the cure is so. I believe everyone's cure is their own. Mine was H. Yes of course she would get angry with me. And say for fuck's sake come on. And she'd burst into tears at the strain. But her anger and her tears never hid her caring. She took me to a hypnotherapist. She sat outside the room. I had to know she was there. I didn't care who else was there. I didn't need them. I needed her. Right outside the room. I didn't trust the hypnotherapist. He was a doctor. What the fuck did he know. It was all a waste of time. I wanted to go home with H.

Something in me said this is all ridiculous. I understand mental illness. Coming from my family this is no great achievement. But nonetheless I'm still mentally ill. But why do I need her so much? I'm an intellectual. I know I'm far cleverer than her. I've been around the world. I went to UCD. I can speak Afrikaans. I can calculate the stresses in a beam, design a sewage scheme, build you a house, write you a book on any theme. She's a schoolgirl with great tits. Why do I need her? Because. That was the answer.

H and the hypnotherapist cured me. Both with their own magic. I flushed the pills. She never reminded me how much I had needed her. She knew how much I had needed her. But it was just a fact to her, not a weapon in some armoury. She doesn't really have any weapons in any armoury. Which is strange, in a woman descended from generations of soldiers. Or maybe that's the reason. Whatever, she's at peace. No-one can really hurt her except me. She's wise and weary to the ways of the world. She's been there, knows what people are like. If they're good they're good and bad they're bad, she knows the difference.

We went on with our lives.

Things took a big change. And H now gave up a life of attending international trade fairs with sophisticated well turned out and neatly coiffed Irish publishers, like Michael O'Brien of *The O'Brien Press* here, escorted by get-up-and-go Brad Pitt lookalike Irish government officials such as Greg Carley…yes… threw all that away to go back to the West of Ireland. But that's what she did. I suppose high flying got tedious. And that a night in Frankfurt with a bunch of Irish book publishers tends to be the same as…well…a night in Chicago with a bunch of Irish book publishers. But fair play to the hirsute one here, he did publish my first novel, *Here Be Ghosts*. But I know what the reader is thinking. And suddenly something in the look of that photo now makes me think the same. Nah. Couldn't have happened. Could it dear? Nothing like that could in fact have happened with any of those interesting men you jetted round the world with. Writers, journalists, intellectuals. All far from wives and loving home in lonely faceless hotels in foreign cities. Nothing like that could have happened then, could it dear? Nah. Of course not.

"Well certainly not with Michael O'Brien anyway", I heard H mutter as she went over the proofs of this here book.

UP THE MOUNTAINS

ANOTHER ESCAPE FROM THE SOUTH SIDE. H changed her style dramatically, both life and hair. Back in the West of Ireland we had a new and different child in tow. Older one in College now. Or as he would phrase it, putting himself through college. I suspect he's working on his Misery Memoir out there in Abu Dhabi. In his luxury apartment. Or maybe he only works on that when he's back in Dublin. In his multi million Rathmines house. Did it all himself. Had to. His parents were hopeless.

Our new child went to the local school. Hated it. She was mocked for her Dublin accent. By the teacher. We started a horticultural products business and never worked so hard in our lives. A lot of going up mountains for materials. Operating machines. Packing stuff. I suppose it did ok but after a couple of years I looked at the situation and wondered if we were too old for all this. We were. It was also taking up a lot of writing books time. And whilst that might have been good for the literary world, it wasn't so for me.

BACK IN CANADA

FOR REASONS THAT NOW appear obscure, restlessness no doubt, we went back to Canada around this time. Lived in Toronto, and took the child to school on the old fashioned streetcars that still ran then. In recent times they've been replaced with sleek new LUAS-type vehicles. And those who want to run around on the picturesque old versions will have to go to San Francisco, the city which bought them off Toronto. To keep the tourists amused, one supposes. Strange that, one modern city buying another modern city's junk. But the tourism industry does do things like that, and cities become stage sets for our fantasies and dreams.

Another photo here reminds me that I went to the zoo. And here it was in Toronto Zoo that, despite having lived in Africa, I saw my first zebras. There wasn't much wildlife in my part of Africa. Apart from some of the people.

After Toronto we went to rural parts. A house in the woods by a lake. I drank beer and H drank wine. Lots, I suppose. And we looked into the past and wondered about the future.

Both seemed unclear.

We went back to Ireland, and County Mayo.

49 YORK ROAD, DÚN LAOGHAIRE

IT WAS PROBABLY something to do with the air in County Mayo, but H now had two more babies in quick succession. Well it was either the fresh air or the duck eggs, which my Mayo friend Paul Smith says are very good for the sperm count. He should know. Once had a smallholding on Aran Islands. A bloke has plenty of time out there in winter to count his sperm.

Whatever the reasons, she was popping them out. And her history, as us consultants say, dictated that she would go to a decent proper hospital. That really wasn't possible because we wanted the babies born in Ireland. But as Plan B we sort of set up a half home in Dublin again so that she could to Holles Street. Sorry about that, Mount Carmel.

Long years and many pages ago two schoolgirls came into the Bamboo Coffee Bar in Dún Laoghaire. One I married, and one I didn't. The one I didn't marry was H's lifelong friend Ken. Their loyalty to each other continually amazes me. That amazement could be because I have former lifelong friends who stabbed me in the back. Ken herself had also married very young, but it hadn't worked out that well. She was now living up the Wicklow mountains with her partner Pat Hayes. Pat was one of Ireland's top sound men in film and TV. Probably the top. If you hear birds chirping and tweeting in Éamon de Buitléir documentaries, that's Pat. He was there somewhere in the background putting little microphones up their arses. And Ken had become a leading make-up artist for films. And H was administrator of an important trade organisation. They were all actually quite successful. I'm not sure where I fitted in, or what I was doing hanging round with such luminaries. A sort of adopted writer-in-residence to a group of successful media people? Oh well. Better than being a writer-in-residence to Leitrim County Council I suppose.

Thinks! That writer-in-residence thing is a lot of old bollocks really. Writers should be poor, neglected and unsung. And solitary. Kept away from normal citizens and particularly from other writers. They can swarm, and become unpleasant. And shag each others spouses. I don't mix with writers. I don't like writers. They are a self opinionated and self seeking bunch. Yes, that word self comes into it an awful lot. Miserable, introverted, racked with bitterness and memories of past wrongs, mostly imagined, writers are spectral creatures on the fringes of society, spectral haunted creatures. Haunted by a terrible fear of failure and knowledge of their own mortality. And a sense of inevitable and existential doom.

Believe me, I know.

Conveniently enough, for H and myself anyway, Ken had inherited a very nice house in York Road. A very organised and practical person, Ken had split this into flats. One for her son, one for herself and the rest for renting out. Make up artisting can be up and down as a source of income. It's either feast or famine. Writing much the same. Worse. Veering between only almost starving and critical, perhaps Bono demanding something to be done.

The flat which had been Ken's own personal residence was particularly luxurious and elegant, she being a particularly luxurious and elegant sort of person. With much better taste than me. Strange that, seeing as it was me that went to UCD School of Architecture. Though maybe not strange at all, maybe those two facts are connected in a different way.

So in we moved. And wandered round in awe. Like American soldiers from trailer parks in Arkansas, gobsmacked in one of Saddam's palaces in Iraq. Though Ken's of course was far more tasteful.

We settled in, but flittered back and forth to Mayo. Not to keep the sperm count up, no. In fact significant efforts were now being made to keep the sperm count down as low as possible. We moved around a lot because it was in us, we had become gypsies. Totally incapable of settling anywhere. Inept. Indecisive. In love. In debt. In someone else's apartment.

Something had to happen. It did. I grew a beard, and we bought a house in Dalkey.

York Road to Whites Villas

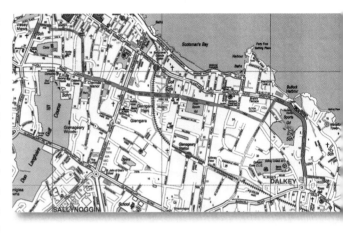

IT IS FIVE IN THE MORNING in Mayo. I always start work at five in the morning, creature of habit. H is next door in our other house, going back to sleep. She always wakes to my departure at four thirty in the morning. No words are spoken. We play with each others toes with our toes, for awhile. Toes are a very erogenous zone, when you get to a certain age. Something to do with where they've been. Their closeness to the earth and paths they've walked and places stood. There's a lot to be written about toes, really. There's a lot more to be written about H's toes. Probably a lot more than I will write. But when I was a shoe fetishist…haven't we all…no…oh well…when I was a shoe fetishist H would wear high spikey heels with strappy things around her toes and ankles. They weren't very comfortable, but she had to do what she was told. Because when I was a shoe fetishist she was a must-do-what-I'm-told fetishist. Yes of course this carry-on is typical of a sado masochistic relationship. But what are words, apart from embarrassing. And in case the wrong impression is given be assured that H only ever wore rubber boots for working in the horticulture. But they were the same toes. Inside those rubber boots. And of course I wasn't a shoe fetishist when we were in the horticulture game. I didn't care what she wore as long as I could go to sleep. Neither of us were any sort of fetishist then, too tired. But we recovered. And I became an I-want-you-all-in-black fetishist. Wear-black-woman-it's-an-order. So she would wear black from skin to coat for weeks. Silently, biding her time. At a particular point that I would not anticipate she would suddenly appear in white. Or multi coloured. And go about her business, silently. Nothing would be said about the change. But her silent defiance would be very erogenous. Much more erogenous than toes, in all honesty. Yes we are a very very kinky couple really. But this is a before-the-watershed book, an all the family reading book, so I'll write no more about where all that led. I wouldn't be allowed anyway. H is very shy about these things. With bloody good reason. It was all her fault. She led me on. You know the way that women are. And anyway I'm in a bit of a hurry now. Anxious to finish up here, other work is piling up around my ears.

So hurry out the door of number 49. And down the steps and pause and look around. York Road is, historically speaking, a terribly staid sort of street, many grand effusions of Victorian enthusiasm punctuating the built environment. We have The Birds' Nest, a Mrs Smyley's home, a former orphanage. Personally I feel it was an institution intent on turning little shoeless catholic waifs into little protestants with shoes. But no harm in that. I'm half protestant, never did me any harm. And anyway whacking great buildings like the Presbyterian Church nearby take some filling of a Sunday. They need every protestant they can get. York Road, a protestant street for a protestant people. Also here in this most protestant of Kingstown's streets was the Kingstown Grammar School. It was later to evolve in some horrible mutant way into Newpark in Blackrock. My older son went there. There was a drug and sex problem. But that was the teachers. Whatever, both Grammar School and Mrs Smyley's are no more, but happily the Presbyterian church remains. And a nice class of motorcar gathers there for Sunday services. Presbyterians these days wouldn't live near York Road in a fit. There has been ominous and irreversible changes. Not least that further up the road is the headquarters of the Irish Christian Brothers. Though a much maligned body really. If it weren't for them I wouldn't bother writing books. Few enough Irish would be able to read and write. Worth considering.

So, considering all that, turn sharp right. Those particularly interested in architecture could, firstly, stroll to Cambridge Terrace, built in 1865 and one of the town's first examples of the use of machine made brick. OK, maybe a bit specialised for the general reader. So those more interested in the love story I am writing here could forget about that, and head with me now into the back streets of Dún Laoghaire. I like them, the Coronation Street atmosphere. Of course back before their partial gentrification it was even more redolent of back to back. Washing lines hung across lanes where children played weird traditional street games among bust open bin bags and women huddled in gossipy groups. Moaned about their men. Men who were mostly down in the Harbour Bar. Well they won't go there now. That pub is empty dereliction and a haunted looking place. And the ghosts who haunt it are dead working men.

We're in Northcote Avenue, but won't be here for long. Nip around the corner and we arrive in Cross Avenue. Opened up in 1905, it's not the most imaginatively named streets, perhaps thought up by the same bloke who decided on the name Link Road for Glasthule.

But it does have a very nice street sign. And a fairly ordinary one. These street signs tell many tales, of times that care and times that don't. They've gotten utilitarian in modern times. But no matter what, and particularly around this neighbourhood, they tell a story.

The neighbourhoods around York Road were a fantastic charivari. A painting by Lowry, with additional features touched in by Hieronymous Bosch. The partial gentrification has put a bit of a stop to all that. Part of that partial gentrification is my sister Ann The Artist. One of my five sisters. She used to live in a corpo flat near here. Her grandfather who had the mansion in Dalkey would turn in his grave…if he wasn't already in constant revolution due to the rest of us. In actual fact the corpo flats behind these brick walls are very nice. The original old houses have in recent years all been drastically rebuilt inside. Probably a downside is that the rebuilt flats are too small for families by modern criteria, and so the demographics round here can be a bit strange. Generally there are an awful lot of single people.

Many of whom are very very strange indeed. I do get the impression of a housing department dumping ground for waifs and strays. And in many cases the ominous phrase care in the community jumps into mind. The virtual absence of small children and traditional couples is quite eerie really. If that city in the film Blade Runner had suburbs they'd probably be very like this. Eerie and quiet. Though my sister Ann tells me that sometimes a resident will go berserk, and howl to the moon through the night. But should I worry. I'm far away then. Playing with H's toes.

Yes that's what it says on the street signs now, Convent Road there to our left. In early years this was known as Paradise Row, which has a nice ring to it. We cross it here as it leads down to the town and the corner

where a woman by the name of Vera used sell fish of a Friday. The fish stand was connected to the Shorthall family, go back yonks in the town. I knew one of them, had pints with him in the Purty Kitchen. A security man in the Motor Yacht Club on the West Pier. He was murdered by intruders.

Welcome to Ireland.

Paradise Row.

A lot of this land around here was associated with the convent. The nuns were Dominicans. When I think of Dominicans…which is not actually that often…but when I do I always think of Sister Mairead in Drogheda in Sienna Convent. She's the boss there. I met her a year or so back, researching something for a book I was on. And I wrote a poem about her. Sent it to her for comment. She phoned me up and said oh please don't publish that. Please. Please. So I said I wouldn't. She said oh thanks, now I can sleep at nights. So I didn't publish the poem. And Sister Mairead sleeps at nights. Though I actually don't know what she was worried about. There was nothing erotic or suggestive or compromising or likely to cause alarm in Central Control back in Dominican World HQ. It just said how lovely she is. Because she is. All spirit and grace and close to God. More women should become nuns really. The world needs them. And has forgotten that it needs them. Those women all spirit and grace and close to God.

Oh Yes. I know that a goodly number of my women readers are now muttering yeah, you become a bloody nun then mate.

Well let me tell you girdles. I wouldn't mind being a nun, but I doubt they'd let me enter. Come to think of it, in actual fact I feel that maybe I was a nun, but back in the fifteenth century. Yes, it's all coming back to me now. My family put me into the nunnery because of that incident with the boy who looks after the cows. My name is Heloise. At two in the morning I sing in the chapel. But no-one hears the song in my heart.

Could've happened.

So, moving right along.

Cross Avenue ends at the Patrick Street junction. Though there is a small nameless section of street which may very well be an orphan of the main, it's hard to tell. A glance down Patrick Street as I pass. Up this end it seems to be mostly closed down, but it was a lively street in times gone by. Dún Laoghaire's first supermarket was here, Connollys. And the bloke in Glasthule who cuts what remains of my hair is a cousin of that family. And he cuts my hair just as his father cut my father's hair. God we're a tight knit bunch, Dún Laoghaire natives.

Connolly's is now a restaurant. Alexis. Well in 2009 as I write it's called Alexis. That building has gone through many manifestations. Have to be careful. I write these words for posterity, and for the unnumbered ages and aeons to come, not as a fleeting restaurant guide.

Moving along, and turning right up Mulgrave Street. And soon enough we're back in Corrig Road again. Yes we've passed this way before. But that was way back when. How many years and pages passed? I cannot calculate. I was on my way to the church in Monkstown to get married.  How many years and pages passed since then? How many times did we laugh and cry, make love? And fight, how many times did we fight? Not much, but when we fought we fought. Half way through this book we fought. I walk down Corrig Road and into Eden Road and remember.

It is that time of evening. We are drinking wine, H and I.

This is not the greatest of ideas. There can be conflicting views, about life and that. I've just told her my literary agent in London has emailed me about the novel. Apparently I'm the greatest thing since sliced bread. But both H and I know about the publishing business. We have worked it all our lives. So the news washes over us. We will wait for the cheques. And wait a little more until they clear. And even when we spend the money we will have no particular opinion. We made that money. It is ours. I write the words in the right order. That's my job, it's what I do. And her presence in the night gives me peace and meaning for tomorrow's words. That's her job, the arrangement. Her peace in the night, my words in the right order. It doesn't make me any good, and does nothing for her either. I was born with writing talent, and she was born with tranquility. The separate roles are irrelevant. I am not the writer, and she is not the body of a woman. We are quite beyond that.

It is that time of evening. We are drinking wine, H and I.

We both knew that it was all bollicks. Literature and writing and a few bob in the bank at the end of the day. We both knew that I was only a bricklayer, a plumber, a technician who could put the words together in the right order. We both knew that she was only a small woman born in Portlaoise with heavy breasts and a lovely smile. We both knew that women had liked me and men had liked her. And we both knew, what the fuck, what the fuck. Neither of us were young any more. Her body was not so beautiful. And mine was going on decrepit.  We had graves waiting for us. Alzheimers maybe. Who knows?

Who fucking cares, and fuck them if they do.

It is that time of evening. We are drinking wine, H and I.

It has been a difficult life. We are both hard people now. The only difference is that I am hard and cold and she is hard and warm. There's a reality in us. It was always in me, and always in her too. Don't laugh at me, her eyes said when I met her first. Don't laugh at me, you fucker from Africa. You think you know it all. You've been there, you've done it all, her eyes said, but you haven't been with me. And don't look at my tits like that, that's not where we're at. And she turned away and walked away and I had to chase her for weeks around the fucking town. I had to look for her around Dún Laoghaire. Make an asshole of myself in front of her giggling friends. And get her on her own and say you've got to marry me. And she knew right well she had to marry me, but didn't make it easy.

It is that time of evening. We are drinking wine, H and I.

Something comes up, a difference of opinion, interpretation. H takes offence. I'm not going to be fucking doing with you, she says. This is Portlaoise lingo, she was born in Portlaoise, but I speak fluent Portlaoise and I understand. She gets up from the table and storms to the door. There goes the mother of my children, I realise. There goes my schoolgirl. I watch her. And it's good to see her furious. So good to hear her saying, I'm not going to be fucking doing with you. It's good to see her free of me for awhile. She is her own woman now. I love the woman free of me even more than the woman who is mine. The woman who is mine is too much part of me. Too much in my shadow. Mother of my children. Her breasts in my children's gobs. Washing my socks, cooking my food. She pauses at the door. And I'm not going to be sleeping in your fucking bed tonight, she adds. A parting finality. And she is gone then and I think, god how much I love her. And the empty bed is waiting for her return. And in the morning she reappears and says what was that all about? And neither of us know, so we shrug it away and go about our day.

So, going about our day.

Hudson Road now, we'll nip across there. Past the derelict sportsgrounds of Pres...why is everything derelict these days? Things fall apart, said Yeats, the centre cannot hold. Something like that. I remember circuses in that field there, but I never liked circuses. My aunt in London hated them too. I had a record then, Ravel's Bolero, and I played it for her, continuously. Sort of setting the atmosphere. For that trip. We were planning. To Yugoslavia. Then she said one night stop playing that bloody record, it reminds me of circuses. So I stopped playing the bloody record and there was silence between us for decades. And then she left me her house in Kerry. And the circles were all circled, and the squares squared, and a line drawn under.

Across Albert Road. Yes we've been here before, I was heading down to nursery school. It seems a while. But let us not dwell on the past. Just as the dead bury the dead, so let my words my words.

Hard to believe but another, another derelict site. In this supposedly most prosperous area of Dublin. Here in leafy Elton Park, massive hoardings. It seems to have been like this for years. Things fall apart...true for you, Yeats, the centre cannot hold. The Second Coming coming, I suppose. Well, I don't suppose. Suppose is not the word. I know. I know about all that, that darkness on the way. Myself and Blake and Yeats, I keep good company.

Máire Ní Chearbhaill lived right there, with her father. Right here in the house which stood on the derelict site. Her father Breandán was a famous local historian of Dún Laoghaire. And Máire worked as an editor for me. I met her through H, they worked together in Veritas. Máire was an editor of religious books, and H was a secretary to religious men. Catholic communications men. Joe Dunn. Liam Swords. She was the female flesh in the office. And I suppose H coming in fresh and fragrant in the mornings gave pause for thought about the meaning of priestly celibacy. But not that much. They were committed men. Committed to communications. God's message. All that. I wonder how well that went. Joe Dunn is dead. His family were big fish merchants in Dublin. Liam Swords lives on. His nephew runs a tyre company in Ballina. Gave him two hundred euro a few weeks back for new tyres. Had to. My NCT was up. Time passing, and thoughts of tyres. And the National Car Test. And times remembered and the voluptuous secretary bouncing up the stairs in Veritas in Abbey Street. "Good Morning Father Joe", she says. "Good Morning H", he says.

Catholic Communications.

God's message.

Castlepark Road now. And Hyde Road over the way. That Hyde Road junction was notoriously haunted when this was a place where farm lanes met. I don't remember this place when farm lanes met, but older people told me so. I don't know why, I suppose it's an old area, with old messages in the soil. And there may very well have been a gallows here, handy for miscreants from the walled enclave of Bulloch down the way. I actually haven't the remotest idea.

Cherish that sentence.

It may not reoccur.

I'm an admirer of Douglas Hyde. And I'm sure he cares a lot about that in his grave at Tibohine. Which I pass every week or so and used to salute like a soldier to an officer. "Why is Da saluting ?" the kids would ask and H would grin and shrug and give no answer.

I don't salute no more, and I sometimes wonder why. Perhaps because the kids are grown up and gone. And there's no-one in the car to perplex with my eccentricities. They certainly wouldn't perplex H. Though if I started acting normally she might get very confused.

Despite my admiration for the folklorist and founder of the Gaelic League, my route from here doesn't go along Hyde Road. It's dreary enough anyway, apparently inhabited by modern day editions of Hugh Leonard's Mr Drumm. They have that look about them. Tight arsed time serving civil servants and the like. The numbers of their pension plans tattooed onto the wives' buttocks. So we'll leave them be and turn left down Castlepark Road instead.

And I don't believe it! Yet another derelict site where once was the garden centre under the stern Ms Roseingrave to whom I sold horticultural products in distant days. But I've said my say about the dereliction, and move on. To the left here in number two lived my great great great aunt, Elizabeth Clinton. There's genealogy. My grandmother's great aunt. From Drogheda, she was daughter of William Clinton, a butcher of that town. And is buried in the Chord Cemetery there. But that's derelict and closed and I could never get in to see her grave. Wealthy enough, the butcher had a few bob, she travelled, worked as a schoolmistress betimes, and was an artist of some talent. I have her paintings. Not on my walls, because they are heavy and victorian and would only serve to increase my natural gloom, but securely tucked away. My Will directs them to my children. A bit of Victorian gloom in their frivolous lives won't go amiss.

Elizabeth, or as she signed herself Eliza, but never Liz...Eliza also owned a house across the road at the bottom, number three of Neptune Terrace. A sombre looking red brick house. We're heading along that way now, but turning to the right and up Ulverton Road towards Dalkey. Ulverton takes the name, trust me on this, from the surname Yelverton, a family that owned quarries along here. A scion of the same Yelvertons built the port of Fremantle at Perth in Western Australia. The surname Yelverton derives from that of a town in Devon, and the Irish family of the name became the Lords Avonmore. My Coonan/Conan stonemason ancestors were lackeys or varlets or followers in some way of the Lords Avonmore, working for them in Mayo on the restoration of Ballintubber Abbey. The Fine Gael politician Noel Coonan, a TD of Tipperary shares these roots. As indeed does my cousin Mary Conan White, a Green TD in Carlow.

A lot of information buried in the name of a single road.

The roofs of *Our Lady's Manor* depressing enough on our left. I often think that some activists, perhaps akin to animal rights fundamentalists, should break into those sort of places and release the old from their unnatural imprisonment. I  often think, but it probably won't happen. Though history no doubt will look back on nursing homes in much the way we view workhouses. With distaste, and bewilderment. Though of course that will be in the same time that the old are being disposed of by painless injection.

Castle Park School to our right. The house once the home of Arthur Perrin, a kinsman of my family, quarry owner. He went bankrupt. It figures. My sister Louise taught swimming in the school there. Kept herself very fit. Ate well. Exercised. Died suddenly and young of a freak condition. A prayer for her as I pass, thoughtful. And onward now to Dalkey, still thoughtful. Nothing much more to say about Ulverton Road. The tram route. In a Dalkey pub once I met an old man who told me that when he was a boy he knew an old man long dead who's job was to mind the extra horses that would be fixed to the horse trams…to help pull them up this hill. Those men dead now. It's the way of things. For the tellers of stories and the told alike.

And so into Carysfort Road.

White's Villas around the corner.

9 WHITES VILLAS, DALKEY

TO SAY THAT WE HAD EVOLVED a bad credit record is…well… precise. But that is then and this is now and all the banks who threw us out their doors have themselves gone bust. So bugger you mates. Serves you bloody right. What goes round comes round. Up yours. You had it coming you bastards. And may you all rot in hell.

Exactly, the reader is correct. I do not do forgiveness.

Due to the impaired financial situation it had to be H and not me or even us who bought the little house in Dalkey. The day the mortgage came through she phoned me up and said 'I've got the key, they've given me the key'.

"They must be mad" I said.

"Who gives a shit", she said, "I've got the key.'"

We moved in.

Our God had smiled on us. But in a sardonic way. Because just after buying it, and every penny spent, my aunt in Kerry died and left me her house. On the side of a mountain overlooking Kenmare Bay. With a stream and woods and things like turbary. It was beautiful. Yes it did have a downside, in that it was surrounded by Kerrymen, but this was one nice gaff. As us homeless people tend to say. Us homeless people who now had three houses. One in Mayo, one in Dalkey, and one in Kerry. And four dependant children, and not one…single…penny.

We reviewed the situation. Many times in life we had reviewed our financial situation. This usually took the format of H drinking a couple of bottles of wine, bursting into tears and being carried off to bed. And me lying there beside her, plotting. How dare those fuckers make my beloved cry, I'll screw the bastards. Which I invariably did. Bailiffs? Hah, I wave my genitals at your bailiffs! That is an expression I learned from the Latvian ex-wife of my brother-in-law. I really don't understand it. It only seems to make sense in the context of the ex in ex-wife.

I'm none too sure about Latvians.

It was decided to apply a more positive review of the situation. We were heavily in debt to a criminal organisation, now known to be the *Irish Nationwide Building Society*. Or should I have written that the other way around? Anyway, there was a mortgage to be paid on the Dalkey residence. It might have been a former corpo house in a back street, but Dalkey does residences, not houses. Our income was minimal, and the horticultural business had been run down. I'm particularly good at that aspect of business.

So there was nothing for it. I'd have to work. H was busy, couldn't work, breast feeding what seemed to be half of Dalkey. I lashed out a few books, guide books and the likes, and a novel, revived our publishing business, and published the few books. The guide books. Someone in London has that novel. Still. Pending. But anyway in no time at all we had enough liquidity to commute between our three houses. Few months here, few months there, few months back again. I renovated the Kerry house, built more at the Mayo house. Put a bathroom into Dalkey. Amazing the power of words. Particularly when you put them down in the right order.

And so it was in Dalkey that we brought up the two new children. I'm glad of that. Dalkey is essentially my home town. My children were the fourth generation of the family in the town. I like that continuity. My mother's family had been associated with the place for a few hundred years. My book *Grandfather's House* deals with all that. Not that my mother approved at all of us living in Whites Villlas. A glance here at the said grandfather's house may suffice to explain why she took such grave exception to our bijoux property.

Snobbish? My mother's people? Never.

Dalkey is a very strange place. Image wise. It's not at all what it seems, or like it is portrayed in the media. Trendy expensive home of the famous, rattling with celebrities. Yes there is some of that and, at least before the demise of the economy, there was a lot of nonsensical restaurants and pubs. And a lot of people spouting nonsense in them. Finnegans is perhaps best avoided in that regard. Even today in these hard times. But on the whole Dalkey is a fairly normal and ordinary place, people going about their business. It's just the web and the weave of the normal Irish style fabric of society.

Down in White's Villas it must be said that we were sort of different, us residents. The fabric of society was in some stress. Nothing to do with the houses. Not bad little concrete houses, built on the former allotments associated with the tramway cottages. It's actually all about trams in that part of Dalkey. The allotments were wrapped round the old tram stables, so to speak, and the cottages for the tram workers ranged along two streets behind. On top of all this the actual construction of the villas had been orchestrated in the 1930's by a tramways man, Inspector White. The initial residents had been rehoused from the godawful cottage slums up along Tubbermore and Sorrento Roads.

Dalkey grew up strange. There was no right or wrong side of the tracks. Originally it was just a mass of huts and cottages something like the outskirts of modern Sao Paolo. It was essentially a shanty town for quarry workers, spread out all over the rocky coastline around the ancient town. Gradual change came with an influx of better off people, buying up land and building large houses in the midst of the shanties. And thus it happened that the rich and poor lived alongside. My own great grandfather demolished a street of cottages in front of his house Monte Alverno. He owned them, but said he didn't want to be a slum landlord. Built a nice garden on the site instead. Not at all sure what happened to the residents. They certainly didn't come to Whites Villas, because that was way back in the 1860's, and there was no-one building anything along those lines in those days.

It changed in later years. One cottage family that did come to the villas was that of the parents of the writer Hugh Leonard. A man I admired, I doubt he returned the compliment. My mother was a neighbour of his mother up in Sorrento, the one in her mansion, the other in a cottage. He didn't think much of the old Dalkey upper crust, or so he told my aunt. Rudely. But then he was rude to everyone regardless of social background so I suppose it didn't matter. He and I exchanged correspondences about various things historical. Not the easiest of correspondents, things would frequently break down. Then he would lose his cool and send one of his 'kiss my ass' postcards. He'd had them specially printed. There's planning ahead for a lifestyle.

It was a delicate arrangement, that fabric of society thing in the villas. Many of the residents were descendants of those earlier transposed slum dwellers. And it showed. Whereas on the other side of the street a lot of the people in the tramway cottages were children and grandchildren of tramways workers. These were a cut above us Whites Villas lot. The cream of the cream, and that showed too. There was a big social divide.

Some of the families on our wrong side of the divide were more functional than others. Nights were sometimes rent with screams of women and the barking howls of drunks. This on top of the normal screams of middleclass women and the barking howls of middleclass drunks going home from the *Queens Pub* behind.

Yes there were feuds and long memories among many of the resident families. Bottles could be hurled at walls, that sort of thing. And in one of the houses was a witch, she only came out of night. And would put the heart across you by her sombre passing. There were allegations of dark deeds in a particular house. Of incest and dead babies, stabbed with knitting needles. The police took over that house. Ripped up the floorboards and dug the garden. But the allegations remained just that. And life went on.

H and I fitted very well into this ambiance. We understood witches. And the dark corners of the human soul. We fitted in well but we did move a lot, rotating with the children between our three houses. All was well. For quite awhile. For years. But then things went pear shaped in the financial sense. Again. We were well used to that. H entered into negotiation with the criminal organisation who were threatening her with eviction. Went in to HQ to plead her case. But Michael Fingleton made her cry. I hated that. So I put a curse on him. I had lived in Africa. And I had called my business after the Irish goddess of darkness. Trust me, I know that stuff. He would have no joy. Yes he'd have a good pension eventually. But he'd have no joy. And would end his days miserable. Wearing a silly hat. Open your newspapers. Be careful of my curse.

Fingleton safely cursed, it was decided to jump before being pushed so we sold up in Dalkey. It was a wrench. I had done a lot of work on the house. When we had moved in there was a wc in a cubbyhole and a tap over a sink in a shed like kitchen. There was electricity, but the original gaslight fittings were still about the place. And yes, this was in the last decades of the 20th century, birth years of the celtic tiger. It seemed the economic progress since the nineteen thirties had left little mark on the likes of Whites Villas. I put in a bathroom, and a kitchen. And wood panelling in the bedroom for H to sit against in bed, thoughtful. Even melancholy. And why wouldn't she be? She and I make up a thoughtful and melancholy couple. And I'm not sure that either of us believes that much in happiness.

Yes, leaving Dalkey was a wrench. And not only for myself. I felt I was somehow letting down those generations of Dalkey ancestors. Abandoning the town to the blow-ins, to the dross of celebs and media wankers. But, abandon it we did. And then, to make a decent blaze of all our boats, we sold the Kerry house. And moved with the young children back to base camp in Mayo. Our older son was in TCD, and independent. Albeit a sort of imposed independence. I had thrown him out, put all his stuff on the doorstep of Whites Villas. And he had gone about his business. The makings of the lad! Now earns half a million dollars a year in Abu Dhabi. The older girl was still at school, in Coláiste Íosagáin. But said she wouldn't come back to Mayo with us in a fit. And, brought up bilingual, she also said the Irish-language version of not coming back to Mayo with us in a fit. It meant the same. So we had to leave her behind in Dublin. We boarded her out with a friend who had four sons and no daughters. A sort of fostering. Ancient Irish tradition. Families depositing their children with others of a vastly different social background. In our case the fostering family was that of a chartered accountant. Couldn't get much different than that.

The financial mess had arisen because our focus had gone elsewhere. We were off the planet. In a different zone. And we actually weren't that bothered about the three houses and the poverty. We had lost our grip. The only thing unneglected was our children. We had always looked after them well. It's always been in us, that centre. Perhaps because of the lost child in America. Or just because that's the way we are. And after all they are our pension. (He writes more in hope than expectation). But overall and in general the survival systems had unravelled. Blokes wanted to repossess the car. I wasn't in the mood. I chased them down the road with a brick. If I'd still had the gun of African days I might have shot them. That was the edge I was on. They set the Guards on me. But Dalkey Guards don't give a bugger about someone attacking repo guys with a brick. Dalkey Guards are there to protect the likes of Pat Kenny from burglars. It looks bad if Pat Kenny gets burgled. If someone attacks repo guys with a brick it just looks like Whites Villas. Ireland runs on PR. Fantasy. And illusion. But I don't really care. I care about my own life. And in my own life the bottom line is they didn't get the car. Because from then on H and I would park it in back lanes of the town to avoid the repo guys. It was a pain in the neck. Why do we have to hide the car, the kids asked.

Bad men want to take it away, we told them.

That planet we were living in, the different zone, that was all about our personal relationship. And no, I'm not auditioning for a job as a counsellor in *Accord*, I'm just treading delicately. H will read this book in manuscript, very soon. A very large blue pencil in her hand. Well you can scrub that out for a start, she'll say. And that. And that. I don't want people knowing that, she'll say. And for fuck's sake, is nothing sacred? And of course everything between me and her is sacred. And of course I'll do as she asks. I always have, that's the deal. So if these next two paragraphs here look a bit awkward, and not quite coherent, it's the fault of the censor, not the writer.

Dalkey was the strangest of times. We had been married for well over twenty years, but had re-met each other in the…where am I going with this sentence…in the personal relationship area of life. See, I told you I was a professional writer. I can find the words. In the old hippieish days I might have written something like we had a heavy sex thing going down. We had. But these were not the old days, we were mature adults. We had re-met each other in the personal relationship area of life. And had a heavy sex thing going down. But things were different now. If there were words to write all this I'd surely write them. I am a master of words, this is my trade but still, there are no words for those years when we lived in Dalkey. Or none that I will write down here for sure. I wouldn't be let anyway.

I suppose Dalkey was fun. Looking from this distance. Now that there's a shedload of money in the bank. But this was a difficult time. Our togetherness was complete. Neither of us could escape from the other. The notion just couldn't arise. I think I wanted to, sometimes. I know she did, a lot. But we were the one unit, and there was no disentangling. We had been together a very long time. Been through a lot of things together. We had moved beyond what people know as love. Beyond love there is no longer separate people. There's a sinister sort of oneness in that place. That's not a great place. It's worth visiting, but you don't want to stay there forever. There's postcards from that place in H's picture here.

9 THE BEECHES, MONKSTOWN VALLEY

BACK IN MAYO things calmed down. Mayo is a very calming place. Maybe over the years of back and forth we had absorbed something. Something in the air that manufactures Mayo people. It was almost our real home. Our older daughter had gone to school there, years before. And now our younger family were following her. We didn't actually have many friends in Mayo. But then we didn't actually have many friends in Dublin either. Perhaps because of our peripatetic lifestyle. Here today and gone tomorrow. Though I think also people were afraid of us a little. Because we were rather strange. Or maybe that's all shit. Maybe we were just a closed up couple, the world our enemy. And of course there was also the factor that when new people came into one or other of our lives we'd tend to bounce them against the other for approval. Hard for new people to pass that double test.

After a year or so we made another foray back to the south side. Back there our older daughter was finishing school. It wasn't that we'd abandoned her in Dublin. Just left her behind. She'd been safely fostered out with friends. Mind you, her chartered accountant foster parent had, in the interim, done his sums and run away with a younger woman. Set up home with her a few south side roads away. Though a year or so later he made a few more profit and loss calculations and went back to his wife. None of this phased our older daughter. She remained calm. And she and H had stayed close and thick as thieves. So it was decided to go back to Dublin for her Leaving Certificate. Parental support. All that.

We rented a house in Monkstown Valley. This was within spitting distance of our old haunts. A place of ghosts. Almost precisely at the entrance to Monkstown Valley from the Monkstown Road is where I'd stopped my van some twenty something years before. Because a woman I had seen about the place was walking along, slowly and thoughtfully and kicking leaves. It was Milly. I had got out and talked to her. She thought I was mad. A very good judge of character.

But mad or not I had remained friends with her throughout the years. We'd kept in touch. But it was very different now. She and I and H were different people now. And H and I together were different too. We'd left some things behind. And tended not to talk of them. They were safe enough in our minds. We were separate people once again. Separate, close.

Monkstown Valley is a toy town of tickety boo houses. And has what is sometimes described as a transient population. The unspoken but correct definition of this is 'old people waiting to die, mixed in with young people renting on a temporary basis'. Every morning I would walk through the maze of apartment blocks and dinky little houses, observing the demographics. On the whole I preferred the older inhabitants. Probably because, recently from Mayo and with Mayo ways, it was my habit to nod and exchange hello's with passers by. Young Monkstown Valley folks responded with quickened footsteps and lowered eyes, whereas those in God's waiting room responded in like kind. I wondered if this was because the older people had grown up in a more civilised world. Or was it because people get more civilised as they get older? The former, I feel. Most Irish people nowadays get more grumpy and bitter as they age. Civilisation is a foreign word.

In Monkstown Valley H minded the children and I plugged along with publishing and writing. I was getting posher by the minute, to the extent that President Mary McAleese launched a book we published. And she was very nice and giggled nervously when we met. I have no idea why. Some

women have the ability to be both intellectual and feminine, others don't. Mary Mac does. And I found her really nice and very different from the other Mary, her predesessor. I'd met that president too, through the publishing business in earlier years. She didn't giggle, neither nervously nor at all. You wouldn't warm to Mary Robinson really, but she did her thing, a woman of her time. Necessary, I suppose.

Being a bit of a radical feminist myself, I understand.

H in Monkstown Valley. At fourteen minutes past five.

Around the Monkstown Road

AFTER DISENGAGEMENT from my former axe wielding best friend I had taken up with a new best friend. An academic, of sorts, I met him through editing a book he wrote. Well, I met him through rewriting a book he wrote. But people like me who edit people's books don't really like to put it like that. It's bad for business to tell academics that they can't put two words or thoughts together in a cogent manner and should give it all up and get a proper job and stop screwing the taxpayer. The book I wrote...oops...edited was then published by *Irish Academic Press*. It dedicated effusive thanks to myself and H. Because she also had a hand in the editing and because the academic lusted after her body. This made a nice change from the former best friend who had lusted after mine and regarded H's body as rather vulgar. Asked me why I liked fat women. I don't know. I do like fat women. Not that H was ever particulary fat, just has curves. And I like her regardless.

The new best friend had a country cottage. H and I would visit there, he discussing arcane matters with me and lusting after H's body. No flattery to her really, he being pretty indiscrimate about bodies to be lusted after. At a book launch function in Dublin he groped my son's girlfriend's arse. And she to have gone to Mount Anville.

But nonetheless, things were ok, friendship wise. Then Osama Bin Laden intervened. And my new best friend and I fell out over 9/11. My new but very soon to be another former best friend phoned me up on the day and said well you've got to see their point. The suicide plane guys. No. I didn't have to see their point. I had lived in America. I like America and Americans. I have a child buried in American earth. It's sacred to me, that little bit of earth. And on the 9/11 day my son was working in New York. He works in finance and in his business hung around places like the World Trade Centre. And there but for the grace of God. Etc.

So I put down the phone and would never talk to him again.

End of story.

I had gained a new former best friend.

No, not quite end of story. My new former best friend's book was reprinted a few years after. I snuck into a bookshop, had a look at it. Of course I knew, by instinct. Which is why I snuck into the bookshop. To confirm my understanding of the perfidy of mankind and the certainty of betrayal. Yes. The effusive thanks to myself and H was no longer printed. I nodded to myself, feeling wise.

A wise man in Monkstown Valley.

It was a very regular lifestyle there, being a wise man in Monkstown Valley. I would take the kids to school. Just as I had in Mayo. But, instead of driving down country lanes to an isolated schoolhouse in the middle of woods and fields, here we would walk. Out of the little house I would proceed with two small children in tow. Not a particularly young father, I suspect people calculated I was on my second marriage. Well, calculate what they like. They were wrong. The kids would rush ahead and always, always rush through that doorway in the woods. Salvaged from the demolished house *St Grellan's* which once stood on these grounds, it's a very fine piece of stonework. Those columns are each made from a single block of granite. Those kinsmen Coonans I mentioned, they were famous stonemasons, rebuilt Ballintubber Abbey, and built Kylemore Castle. I appreciate stone, it's sort of in the blood.

It's mysterious for little children, that doorway in the woods. A lion and a witch and a wardrobe sort of thing. After *St Grellans* it was the front door of *The Hall School*. Posh, and protestant. A friend of H and myself, Emer Sweeney, a Sacred Heart girl, she says she always wondered at the legs of protestant schoolgirls. So smooth and brown, whereas catholic schoolgirls' legs were red and blotchy. I have no comment to make on that at all. And am not at all sure in what context the subject came up. But Emer knows these things. She worked for Bord Failte. Her grandfather was executed in 1916 for being a signatory of the proclamation. Probably by one of my relatives, most of whom seemed to have been in the British Army.

Emer suspects me of Unionist tendencies.

Out we walk. The tudor-ish house at the entrance to Monkstown Valley is strange. But only to those with long memories. Those with long memories will recall that it was once knocked down and rebuilt the other way around, facing in a different direction. It was also rebuilt without its tudor-ish chimney. No doubt there are answers and reasons. But they are buried with the architect Sam Stephenson in some over designed grave, somewhere. So do not ask or wonder, walk on.

Past the plaque which says 'on this spot the writer Conan

Kennedy met Milly, a great love of his life'. Then on along the main road towards Eaton Square. Out in my Mayo garden now I have half a dozen chestnut trees, several metres high. They have grown from chestnuts that the kids gathered there in those times at Montpelier Parade. H wants to cut them down, they block the light. What does she need light for, I wonder. But I know the answer. To get rid of the darkness.

The oldest of the great Dún Laoghaire terraces, Montpelier dates from the 1790's. It was built by Mr Molesworth Green. Yes, he of the eponymous street in central Dublin. Nice big gloomy houses. Redolent...I knew I'd get that word in somewhere... redolent of upstairs downstairs lifestyles.

At the pedestrian crossing I chat to Jackie Cooke, the lollipop lady. Thing about lollipop ladies, and about women in uniform generally I suppose. They're not really lollipop ladies. Uniforms do not define women, not for me anyway. Girls in suspenders and thongs are not really lap dancers. There's actual people beneath. This tends to be forgotten. The woman-in-uniform concept is a subject for analysis. How society creates its bizarre balancing act between all the different uniforms. The lollipop lady is there to irritate motorists...and the lap dancer there to relax the same motorists... after being irritated by the morning lollipop lady.

I digress. Enough to say the concept is worth investigating. But not by me. The real point is that over the weeks and months of going to school I learned that Jackie Cooke's lollipop uniform hid another person entirely. No, not a lap dancer, but a professional photographer. She had turned to lollipopping as a means to earn a few bob. Get out of the house. And meet interesting blokes like me.

H and I became quite friendly with her. And now one of her mysterious photos of the woods on Dalkey Hill hangs over my ear as I type these very words. Part of the photo is reproduced as frontispiece for this book. The whole photo is a strangely ominous take on the place, and I can't but look at it and see myself as a little boy, wandering there a-wondering. And vaguely nervous of things strange and hidden in the shadows.

Jackie would lollipop us across the road. Then, once there, the kids would tear down Eaton Square and I'd be barely past the walnut tree...yes that's a walnut tree...before they vanished into the school. Bloody ugly building, now that the photo reminds me. How did they get planning permission? Irish language mafia?

No doubt. And with thoughts like that I'd meander on, alone. And take another route back to Monkstown Valley. This time over into Belgrave Square. Meander, and remember.

My friend Helen was brought up in a house directly opposite the entrance to Scoil Lorcáin. She used to work as a masseuse in a joint in Rathmines, and several times I'd dropped her off there. On these journies from Monkstown to Rathmines Helen and I would discuss her breasts, or lack of them. We had that sort of friendship. Never lovers, never would be. Our lives were complex enough already. Modestly endowed, as the saying has it, Helen was always planning to get a job done on them. To enhance her career. But she never did. And later gave up the massage business and became a housekeeper, a factotum. In a big house in Blackrock. *Deepwell.* She then moved to the country with a bloke. And things went pear shaped. So she killed herself. Walked out into the sea and drowned.

I really liked Helen. Never slept with her, just liked her a lot. It's a different sort of liking. Different and in a funny way it's deeper. Yes I almost cried when I heard the news of her suicide. But didn't. I don't cry. I haven't really cried since my daughter died. Which is a long time ago.

Helen's father was a psychoanalyst. He was also a poet. It's a moot point as to which profession he gave the worse name. Rupert Strong. I did not like him at all. And his wife Eithne Strong. I liked her less. A sinister enough couple, they belonged to a coterie of Monkstown shrinks, The Group. It was essentially a cult and, like most cults, it caused an awful lot of damage to the young people caught up in its lunacies.

Helen's sister Rachel also died tragically. She didn't walk into the sea, dramatically, just killed herself in a more gradual way, a lifestyle way. Drug addiction, that sort of way. Men took advantage of her easygoing ways. I didn't. She wasn't really the full shilling. Once climbed into one side of a bed I was in but I exited by the other. It was a peculiar event. But I quite liked her. Not in the same way as Helen, but I liked her. She had that attractive cunning of a child. I trusted nothing about her. That's likeable in a certain sort of woman.

A very talented artist, Rachel was at one time a partner of Graham Knuttel. His name is known. I have seen her described as his 'muse'. But I have linguistic issues with that. To my mind a muse shouldn't really be a better artist than the artist. Then maybe I'm a simple sort of guy. Fact is

Rachel was a far better painter than your man. But history does tend to be written by survivors.

The fun goes on. In recent years there has evolved a Dún Laoghaire poetry prize. In memory of Eithne and Rupert Strong. And those who know nothing, and probably couldn't care, they enter their poems for this. Poems honed and crafted in schools of creative writing. Writers in Residence sort of poems. Poems grant aided by the Arts Council. Mother of Holy Jesus. The lunacy of it all.

Walk on.

The headquarters of Comhaltas dominates Belgrave Square. A very fine building, it in turn dominated by stacks of empty beer kegs up against the gable wall. This is the great thing about being an Irish writer. One merely open one's eyes and records. No need for allegory or metaphor or subtle analysis. It's all there shouting at us. Shouting at us in the mad existence of *The Strong Prize for Poetry*, and in the view of a fine building pulsating with diddleaye music…with stacks of beer kegs against the

walls. Oh but fair play to them, my older daughter learnt her music there. And as I write these words she's the resident diddleaye musician on a cruise liner. And I'm sure I drank the contents of at least one of those kegs. Though not on the same night. But then, I'm not a traditional musician.

This is a musical area. Well, sort of, in manner of speaking. Down there in Osborne Court (of which the walls are red) lived Chris de Burgh, once. Top flat. Trust me. And further along at 17 Seapoint Avenue lived Bob Geldof. Yes these are roads crying out for blue memorial plaques. Crying out of tune in Geldof's case…but whatever.

Walk on. Back up towards the main road now. Long years ago my friend Robin Buick the sculptor lived in the house on the corner here. He wanted H and I to pose for one of his erotic sculptures. He's really a very good sculptor, I reported to her. Tell him to get up the fucking yard, said H, lapsing into pure Portlaoise. She didn't care if he was Michaelangelo. He got up the fucking yard. So there went our chance for immortality in bronze. As students Robin and I had worked in England together. I remember sharing a bed with him. This was the result of an accomodation rather than a sexual crisis. Memories dim, thanks be to God. Walk on. On the opposite side going up to the main road lived Molly Tynan.

A friend of my mother-in-law, she was a woman in her seventies, and toured Monkstown on a bike. Everyone knew her. She was one of those people whom everyone knows. A character. And of course that is shorthand for the fact that no-one knew her at all.

When my mother-in-law died it fell on me to call on Molly to break the news. I went there early in the morning. She was very shocked, and brought me in. I'd never entered the house before. And felt guilty about that. We went upstairs to her chaotic bedsit. She dressed and did her hair. I sat there reckoning I was probably the first man to watch her dressing and doing her hair. The first man for a considerable time, if forever. She had never married. I suspect she fell into the category of women whom my father said would die wondering.

Molly's hair surprised me. It reached her waist. A shock of it, in all senses of the word. I watched as she brushed and combed and twisted it into hanks and chunks and eventually created an elaborate confection of it on top of her head. Dressed and coiffed she reverted back to the woman I knew. The elderly woman whom everyone knew. On her bicycle. Around Monkstown.

We drove away silently. And as I drove I remembered Jenny. A woman I knew in London, had a thing with. Jenny too had very long hair. But she was young and hers was blonde. She was small and neat and my homosexual flatmate Chris used mock her for her breasts. Which were too big for her. Helen would've loved them. But Jenny tried to underplay them. And Chris with that homosexual bitchiness mocked her, for that. I didn't really know where he was coming from, or going. But he later became a big deal in Dublin gay activism. Whatever.

I would watch Jenny in the mornings, confecting her hair to go to work. A serious medical scientist in a hospital, she always wore her hair up in a strict sort of way. Walking speedily down hospital corridors. Brisk and busy. In a white coat like someone in *Casualty*, issuing orders and terrifying lab technicians. With her hair up. As with Molly in Monkstown, everyone knew Jenny too. Or so they reckoned. So they reckoned. But she was an old lady on a bicycle. Except to me.

Walk on. Cross the road, pause. Look down towards the left. Seaview Avenue within spitting distance. My mind drifts back the years. And I think of H. How much I loved her, then. And I think how much I love her now, going back to her in Monkstown Valley.

But I also think of times and people gone. Molly, dead of old age. And Helen, dead, of suicide. And Rachel, dead, of heroin. And Jenny happily married now in London. Four women in this single paragraph. Only one good and happy story. And the rest… tragedy.

Home to breakfast.

The year passed. The older daughter passed her leaving. Passed it well. And went to TCD. And thence to University College London. And became a literary agent. To a writer who'd been struggling for thirty years, this was an irony. But there are many ironies in life. And once she was safely despatched to Trinity we went back to Mayo.

It was more or less exactly the end of the 20th century. Our younger children went back to the local national school, and then to a secondary school in Crossmolina. We did the school runs. We went to the school concerts. We were a middle aged couple, happy. If there is such a state. Our fellow parents were slightly younger than us. But seemed older. Maybe they were just more responsible. With pensions, and that. Lot of good that did them.

The Economic and Social Research Institute
4 Burlington Road,
Dublin 4.
ESRI Telephone: 016671525
To Whom it May Concern
Ms Hilary Kennedy
is a member of our fieldwork team. If you require any further Information please do not hesitate to contact

Interviewer 5987
Number:

I finished building the house, more or less. Bought a fancy car. My mother had died and left me a shedload of money. Not that it made much difference. We lived more or less the same. Just drove faster. H had long left publishing, and got herself a new job. A field researcher with the ESRI. She loved it. I watched her, buzzing happily around with her laptop. She liked to drive alone through the mountains to lonely places. Back at home I would sometimes wonder what she was thinking, out there, driving, alone. I had taught her to drive. But I hadn't taught her to think. That came from herself. So I could get no answer to my wondering. She understood the mountainy people she talked to. And loved them, their foibles and their hopes and dreams. No longer a schoolgirl, she had become wise. Much wiser than the guy who married her. I watched and thought of her and the lives we lived. Some of it I wanted to forget. But remembered most. And particularly I remembered how when she was dying, how I made that deal with God. If she lives, I negotiated, I will look after her. I will live with her for what she wants, and not for what I need. God kept His part of the bargain, and she lived. And I reckon that in Mayo I finally kept mine. It took a while.

KILLALA, COUNTY MAYO

MY PEOPLE HAD LIVED on the south side of Dublin since the 1700's. And before that my mother's family had lived in Dublin city even earlier. Bride Street, places like that. Fishamble Street. They were there when Handel played his music. Hallelujah. Makes me a Dubliner. Might take a bit longer to make me a Mayoman. Those thirty years with a place in Mayo count for nothing. Sounds good, that, place in Mayo. But there is a reality. It has been raining here, as I write these words. The house is a wreck, the roof needs doing. The fact that it is the oldest inhabited house in the town of Killala does not help. Water is trickling down the wall. In another part of the place H lies abed. It is very early. But she is awake, reading. She reads good books, better than I will ever write. She awakes when it rains, because she knows she has to take precautions then. Between her ankles she is steadying a bucket, because the roof is leaking. I actually do have the money to fix it. But I'm very busy. And my son is very wealthy. And I'm no longer that young. Why should I spend my time and money and energy to leave my kids the perfect house? That's not going to happen. It's all about energy efficiency. My energy, efficiency. The place is really just a few ramshackle old 17th century cottages with leaky roofs. An ancient tower and a few modern bits added on. Looks nice in the snow. But don't be fooled, that snow still drips through the slates. Though it has one interesting architectural feature. A plaque which I recently installed over the window of the ancient tower. It tells the story of two lives. The shortened version, in eight characters. The very shortened version I suppose. But then all stories of all lives are shortened versions.

The full length story is the life itself. I know this stuff, I am a storyteller. Two or three years back I wrote a book, a novel, *Ogulla Well,* which sold a thousand copies. Set in ancient Ireland. There is a storyteller, he has no name. And there is a woman, she neither. They go on a journey across Ireland, East to West. The country is a ruined and dangerous place. But they survive. And they learn about good and evil, light and dark.

I keep writing that damn book, been writing it for years. I actually have several unpublished versions written before *Ogulla Well.* I didn't intend to do it again. But reading back through these pages now I know I've written it all over again. I don't think I need to do it anymore. Because this is what I really meant.

That plaque, that date, that 1969. Forty years ago. Holy Mother of God. The year I married the schoolgirl. Oh well. This book the anniversary gift.

So. Whatever. The walk on the south side is over.

It was crazy. Our children think we are weird hippies, and look at us funny. We are funny, a lot funnier than they think. Because yes of course we have our secrets. And some are dark and some are light. But they remain unwritten here. And we'll go with them to graves.

But not quite yet. Thinking of moving to Italy. We like Italy. Spend a lot of time there now. The schoolgirl from Monkstown is still looking good. And this is her a few months back near Monte Carlo. Her kind of place. But that tree? There's one like that in Dillons Park in Dalkey.

Not so sure how good the bloke from Killiney looks. But that's the way. Pictured here in San Remo. A place that works for him. But those palm trees? Remind me of Sandymount Strand. Oh ok. Maybe I write too soon about leaving the real home place.

Dalkey…Sandymount…images in the mind, still.

Dublin south side sort of stuff.

Probably never shake it off.

Children, by Conan Kennedy and Hilary Cox

CK with Alex, Canada, 1977. H with Judy Meg, feeding Clare, Dún Laoghaire, 1987. Hugo and Clare, Kerry. 1995

Alex Brian Ó Cinneide, born 1971. Investment banker, Abu Dhabi. Judy Meg Davina Ní Chinneide, born 1981. Musician, London, (also below right, on left of picture). Hugo Fraoch Kennedy, born 1989. Student, Dublin. Clare Blaithnid Kennedy, born 1987. Retail worker, Dublin.

Also by Conan Kennedy

Fiction

HERE BE GHOSTS

OGULLA WELL

THE COLOUR OF HER EYES

THE NOTTINGHAM ROAD HOTEL

Non-fiction

ANCIENT IRELAND

PLACES OF MYTHOLOGY

IN SEARCH OF DE SELBY

IRISH LANGUAGE IRELAND

Genealogy and History

GRANDFATHER'S HOUSE

CONNECTIONS

Local historical guides to

DALKEY

DÚN LAOGHAIRE

NORTH MAYO

GLASNEVIN CEMETERY

RATHCROGHAN

Conan Kennedy contributes occasional columns to
The Irish Times and *The Irish Catholic*.
A selection of his poetry can be accessed online at
http://deaddrunkdublin.com/poems/conan_kennedy/index.html
He may be emailed at
conan.kennedy@gmail.com

www.conankennedy.com